DISCARDED

POPE
FRANCIS

Look for more fascinating biographies in the series!

Sally Ride

Nelson Mandela

Steve Jobs

George W. Bush

Barack Obama

Hillary Clinton

A REAL-LIFE STORY

POPE
FRANCIS

THE PEOPLE'S POPE

by BEATRICE GORMLEY

ALADDIN
New York London Toronto Sydney New Delhi

ALADDIN

An imprint of Simon & Schuster Children's Publishing Division

1230 Avenue of the Americas, New York, New York 10020

First Aladdin hardcover edition September 2017

Text copyright © 2017 by Beatrice Gormley

Jacket photographs copyright © 2017 by Franco Origlia/Getty Images News

All rights reserved, including the right of reproduction in whole or in part in any form.

ALADDIN and related logo are registered trademarks of Simon & Schuster, Inc.

For information about special discounts for bulk purchases, please contact Simon & Schuster Special Sales at 1-866-506-1949 or business@simonandschuster.com.

The Simon & Schuster Speakers Bureau can bring authors to your live event. For more information or to book an event contact the Simon & Schuster Speakers Bureau at 1-866-248-3049 or visit our website at www.simonspeakers.com.

Series designed by Karina Granda

Jacket and interior designed by Steve Scott

The text of this book was set in Bembo STD.

Manufactured in the United States of America 0817 FFG

2 4 6 8 10 9 7 5 3 1

Library of Congress Control Number 2017941210

ISBN 978-1-4814-8141-0 (hc)

ISBN 978-1-4814-8143-4 (eBook)

To Fr. David Farrell, C.S.C.
And in memory of
Fr. Stephen T. DeMott, M.M.

CONTENTS

CHAPTER 1

A POPE OF SURPRISES

IN SPITE OF THE RAIN, ONE HUNDRED AND FIFTY thousand people thronged St. Peter's Square, in Vatican City, on the evening of March 13, 2013. Many of them had been waiting all day, huddled under umbrellas. Around the globe—in Manila, the Philippines; in Nairobi, Kenya; in Buenos Aires, Argentina—Catholics were gathered in public places. Or they were in their homes and offices, staring at TV screens or hunched over their cell phones. They were all waiting to find out who the new pope would be.

Twitter feeds buzzed with guesses. Most popes of the last two thousand years had been Italian, and the Italian favored this year was Cardinal Angelo Scola, archbishop of Milan. Some felt it was time for a Latin American to head the Roman Catholic Church, and the name they talked about most was Cardinal Odilo Pedro Scherer, archbishop of São Paulo, Brazil. Or perhaps a pope from the United States? An unlikely pick, but still considered a possibility, was Cardinal Sean O'Malley, archbishop of Boston.

All that the people waiting could do was guess, because the 115 cardinals gathered to elect the new pope were locked inside the Sistine Chapel. They were sworn to absolute secrecy, and they had no way to communicate with the outside, other than smoke. For many centuries, at the end of a day's voting, the electors had signaled the results through the chapel's chimney. If white smoke appeared, that meant a pope had been chosen. If black smoke, the voting would continue the next day.

Shortly after seven o'clock, white smoke went up from the chimney of the Sistine Chapel. A pope had been chosen. The mighty bells of St. Peter's began to clang the good news. The Italian crowd shouted, "*Viva il papa!*" ("Long live the pope!") But still no one knew who the new pope was.

More than an hour later, a red-robed cardinal appeared on the central balcony of St. Peter's. He spoke in Latin, the official language of the Vatican, the governing body of the Catholic Church. He announced that the new pope was Jorge Mario Bergoglio (pronounced "Ber-GOAL-io"), to be called Francis.

Who? Most of the crowd in St. Peter's Square had no idea who Bergoglio was, or even what part of the world he was from. The name sounded Italian, but he was not one of the Italian cardinals. The TV commentators, who'd thought they were prepared to explain who the new pope was, stammered. They were learning on the fly, along with the rest of the world.

A Google search revealed that Cardinal Jorge Bergoglio was archbishop of Buenos Aires, Argentina. His nickname there was "Bishop of the Slums." He would be the first pope from South America—in fact, the first from the Americas, as well as the first from the Southern Hemisphere.

More meaningful, perhaps, he was the first pope to choose the name Francis. Saint Francis of Assisi, a thirteenth-century monk, is revered by Catholics, and even by many outside the Catholic Church, as a joyful lover of God's world. He was a rich young man who willingly threw away his possessions and threw in his lot with the poor.

When Pope Francis himself stepped out on the balcony, the onlookers saw immediately that he was not wearing the pope's traditional red velvet ermine-trimmed cape. The cross hanging on the chest of his white cassock was not the papal jewel-encrusted gold cross, but one of plain gray metal.

In the dark, wet square, thousands of cell phones flashed like fireflies to capture this historic moment. Francis paused before speaking, looking out over the vast crowd. He gave the sign of blessing. To the millions of Catholics around the world watching this moment on television, his expression was tender, as if he was greeting his beloved family.

"Brothers and sisters," Pope Francis said in Italian, "good evening." He joked that his fellow cardinals had to go to the ends of the earth to find a new pope. He led the people in the familiar prayers: the Our Father, the Hail Mary, and the Glory Be.

At the end of his brief appearance, Francis blessed the people in a final prayer, as expected. But first, he asked the people to pray silently for *him*. The supreme pontiff bowed low, and a hush fell over the amazed crowd.

Francis had been the head of the Catholic Church for only a couple of hours, but already he had surprised the world over and over.

The Argentinian cardinal Jorge Bergoglio had an Italian last name because his family had emigrated from Italy in 1929. Before that, his grandparents Giovanni and Rosa Bergoglio had owned a coffee shop in Turin, in the northwest Piedmont region of Italy. The Bergoglios were reasonably well off, and their twenty-one-year-old son, Mario, had begun a good job at the Bank of Italy. However, they decided to sell their business and leave Italy. Three of Giovanni's brothers had already moved to Argentina, and Giovanni and Rosa wanted to join them.

In those days, the late 1920s, many Italians thought of Argentina as the land of opportunity. Stretching from the tropics almost to Antarctica, this second-largest South American country was rich in natural resources but sparsely populated. While Italy was suffering through an economic depression, Argentina offered a high standard of living and a good chance to succeed in business.

Furthermore, in Italy the dictator Benito Mussolini had seized power. He turned the country into a police state and would eventually lead Italy into World War II on the side of Nazi Germany. The Bergoglios were eager to escape Mussolini's fascist regime.

Giovanni and Rosa Bergoglio and their son, Mario, made the trip from Genoa to Buenos Aires in 1929 on the *Giulio Cesare*. They had originally bought tickets for an earlier ship, the *Principessa Mafalda*. If they had sailed with that ship, the future Pope Francis's story might have ended before it began.

The *Principessa Mafalda* was a luxury liner, but it was old and poorly maintained. On its last voyage, in October 1927, a propeller shaft broke and punctured the hull. The *Principessa Mafalda* sank near the coast of Brazil, and more than three hundred of its crew and passengers drowned.

But the Bergoglios had delayed their trip, waiting until they could sell their house and coffee shop in Turin. As a result, they made the five-week voyage across the Atlantic safely and arrived at the port of Buenos Aires, Argentina, on February 15, 1929. It was the middle of the summer in the Southern Hemisphere, but Rosa Bergoglio walked down the gangplank wearing her full-length fur coat. Although she must have sweltered in the steamy air, she kept the coat on—the family savings were sewed into its lining.

• • •

The Bergoglios didn't settle in Buenos Aires, the capital city of Argentina, at first, but traveled on up the Paraná River to the city of Paraná. There Giovanni's brothers welcomed the newcomers to their four-story, turret-topped home, which they jokingly called the "Palazzo [palace] Bergoglio." They had built this fine house, equipped with the first elevator in town, with the profits from their paving company.

At that time, Argentina was prosperous from selling exports, including wheat and beef. Its economy was the eighth largest in the world. It seemed that Argentina was on track to become, as some said, "the United States of South America."

However, the Bergoglios' comfortable life in Paraná didn't last long. By 1930 the Great Depression was sweeping over the world. Businesses failed, and workers lost their jobs. European countries no longer had money to buy goods from abroad, including exports from Argentina.

The government of Argentina, weak and corrupt, was unable to steer the country through the crisis. It could not even pay its own employees. In 1930 the army seized control of the government. For more than ten years afterward, the country was ruled by an alliance of the upper class and the military. Elections were held, but they were rigged to get the results the rulers wanted.

Meanwhile, the Great Depression deepened in Argentina as well as the rest of the world. No one had money to spend on paving work, and the Bergoglio paving company went out of business. By 1932, the family was penniless. They had to sell their fine "palazzo" for a tiny fraction of what it was worth. They even had to sell the family tomb. Giovanni, Rosa, and Mario Bergoglio left Paraná and moved to Buenos Aires in search of work.

Luckily, Mario already had a helpful contact in Buenos Aires. On business trips to that city, he had stayed in the guest house of the Salesians of Don Bosco, a teaching order of Catholic priests. Mario had made friends with Father Enrique Pozzoli, who was also his spiritual mentor. And Pozzoli, too, had immigrated to Argentina from Italy, some years ago, so he understood the struggles of immigrants.

When the three Bergoglios arrived in Buenos Aires, Pozzoli took them under his wing. As an important leader in the community, he was able to get them a loan of two thousand pesos, which was enough to buy a warehouse and begin selling goods. Mario could not do the work he was qualified for as a certified accountant, since he did not have Argentinian credentials. But to help support the family, he took any kind of job. He started out making deliveries on a bicycle.

The Bergoglios lived first in Almagro, an Italian working-class section of Buenos Aires. They were devout Catholics, and their social life centered on their church, St. Anthony of Padua. One Sunday in 1934, two of Mario's friends introduced him to their sister, Regina María Sivori. The father of the Sivori family was of northern Italian descent, and the mother, like the Bergoglios, had emigrated from the Piedmont district of Italy.

The following year, in December 1935, Regina and Mario married. By this time Mario had found better work, as a bookkeeper for various businesses. The young couple were able to buy a modest two-story house at 531 Membrillar in the suburb of Flores. Flores was about five and a half miles from the Plaza de Mayo, the central square of Buenos Aires. In the 1930s, Flores was a lower-middle-class neighborhood, with small houses and unpaved streets.

One year after the wedding, on December 17, 1936, Regina and Mario Bergoglio's first child was born at home.

He was baptized Jorge Mario Bergoglio on Christmas Day, by the family's good friend and priest, Father Pozzoli. Jorge's godfather was his maternal grandfather, Francisco Sivori, and his godmother was his paternal grandmother, Rosa Bergoglio.

A year later, Jorge's brother Óscar was born. To help Regina, Grandmother Rosa picked up little Jorge every morning and took him to her house around the corner. From age one to age five, Jorge spent most of his waking hours with Grandmother Rosa.

Many, many years later, two months after his election as pope, in a speech to a huge assembly in St. Peter's Square in Rome, Pope Francis would say that everyone finds their faith through another person. "I had the great blessing of growing up in a family in which faith was lived in a simple, practical way. However, it was my paternal grandmother in particular who influenced my journey of faith."

CHAPTER 2

FAITH, FAMILY, AND SOCCER

IN 1936, THE YEAR OF JORGE BERGOGLIO'S BIRTH, one-third of the residents of Buenos Aires were immigrants. Argentina had been colonized by Spain in the sixteenth century and ruled by Spain until the beginning of the nineteenth, and many of the immigrants were from Spain. But there were also large numbers of immigrants from France, Russia, and Germany—and, most of all, from Italy.

Although the Bergoglios lived in an Italian neighborhood, Mario did not encourage his children to learn

Italian. Spanish was the official language of Argentina, and he wanted them to be fully Argentine. So at home, Mario and Regina deliberately spoke only Spanish. However, Grandmother Rosa and Grandfather Giovanni spoke Italian, and Jorge spent most of his days with them. As a result, Jorge grew up speaking Italian, as well as Spanish, fluently.

Grandfather Giovanni told young Jorge stories from World War I, while Grandmother Rosa introduced Jorge to Italian literature. She read to him from *I Promessi Sposi* (*The Betrothed*), an epic nineteenth-century novel by Alessandro Manzoni. The romantic and patriotic story, the memorable characters, and the portrayal of Christian ideals as well as human weakness made a lifelong impression on the young boy.

Jorge learned from his grandmother that life was a journey of faith. Every day she prayed the rosary, a cycle of prayers to remind Catholics of the main events of their faith. She taught young Jorge to recite the prayers too, keeping track with a rosary string of beads.

Jorge could see how close and real God's love was to Grandmother Rosa, and that she experienced it through Jesus, his mother, Mary, and the saints of the Church. To

Rosa, the saints were dear friends who showed her how to live a Christian life and helped her through hard times. She told Jorge many stories of the saints, including Joseph, Jesus's human father; Saint Francis of Assisi, lover of God's world and the poor; and Saint Thérèse of Lisieux, a young French nun of the nineteenth century.

Grandmother Rosa took Jorge, and later his brothers and sisters, to the Good Friday candlelight procession in Flores. Good Friday, the Friday before Easter Sunday, commemorates the crucifixion of Jesus Christ, and the procession made a deep impression on young Jorge. By the light of the thousands of candles held by worshippers, he gazed at the life-size statue of Jesus on a funeral bier. Grandmother Rosa had the children kneel with her. "Look," she would say. "He's dead, but tomorrow he will rise again."

Once Grandmother Rosa took Jorge to church in a different neighborhood, at the church of St. Francis de Sales. An important event had taken place there in 1934, she explained. Cardinal Eugenio Pacelli, visiting Buenos Aires from Rome, had said Mass there. On that special day, Rosa explained, more than a *million* people had received Communion. And since 1939, that same Cardinal Pacelli had been the present pope, Pius XII.

Grandmother Rosa taught Jorge Christian values, as well as the doctrine and the rituals of the Church. She was scornful of greed for possessions, and for the money that could buy them. "A shroud doesn't have pockets!" she would say. In other words, no matter how much money you have when you die, you can't take it with you.

Later in life Jorge Bergoglio was skeptical of political ideologies, the groups of ideas that explain and justify one political system or another. Some of this attitude may have come from his grandmother. As a young woman in Italy, Rosa Bergoglio had lived through the struggle between two ruthless ideologies, communism and fascism.

The Communists, on the one hand, rejected all religion as ignorant superstition. Soviet Russia, the first Communist country in the world, was a prime example. After coming to power, the Communists had closed churches, arrested priests, and used schools to erase religious beliefs and replace them with atheism, the belief that there is no God.

Mussolini's Italian fascists, on the other hand, wanted to use the Catholic Church as a tool to control the people. Rosa, as a young woman, had been a leader in Catholic Action, working to keep the Church in Italy independent of the government. She often spoke to women's groups. When the fascists shut Rosa out of a lecture hall, she would give her speech from a soapbox outside the building. She even spoke against the dictator Mussolini himself—a dangerous thing to do—from the pulpit of her parish church.

Although Grandmother Rosa was a passionate Catholic, she was able to judge people by what they did, rather than which church they belonged to. This was unusual at the time that Jorge was growing up, because prejudice against Protestants was strong among Catholics, as well as the other way around. The Bergoglios, like most Catholics, did not associate with Protestants.

One day, walking along the street in Buenos Aires with his grandmother, Jorge noticed two women wearing the headdress of the Salvation Army, a Protestant charitable organization. He asked her if these women were nuns. "No, they are Protestants—but they are good Protestants," Rosa told him.

Jorge's parents were also devout Catholics, and they took the teachings of the Church very seriously. For instance, they did not welcome divorced or separated people to their home, and the children were not allowed to visit a friend with such parents. The Bergoglios also avoided associating with people who were atheists or even socialists. However, Mario didn't share the prejudice against Jews that was common among Christians at that time. He made sure Jorge understood that Jesus himself was a Jew, and that Jews had been unjustly persecuted for centuries.

Mario was deeply pious, like his mother, Rosa. At home, he led the family in praying the rosary every night before dinner. On Sundays, the family walked the seven blocks to Mass at the Basilica of San José de Flores, on the Avenida Rivadavia. The Bergoglios were a growing family—besides Jorge's brother Óscar, there was soon a sister, Marta; and then another brother, Alberto.

Inside San José de Flores, rebuilt in 1883 in the Romantic style, there was something to catch young Jorge's attention everywhere he gazed. Under the high-vaulted ceilings, there were gilded altars, colorful statues and icons in every niche, and carved wooden confessional booths along the aisles. A large statue of San José (Saint Joseph), patron saint of families, holding the baby Jesus, looked down from over the main altar.

The church of San José de Flores was not just for Sunday worship. Any day of the week, people could drop in to say a prayer, go to confession, or light a candle. They could stand in reverence before the paintings and statues along the walls, and touch or kiss them, as Grandmother Rosa showed Jorge. That was a way to express love and respect for a saint, a person who helped connect others with God.

A statue of Our Lady of Luján, patron saint of Argentina, stood in the back of the church near the door. It was a copy of a famous statue of Mary, mother of Jesus, which had arrived in Buenos Aires in 1630. It was supposed to be delivered to a settler in Santiago del Estero, hundreds of miles to the northwest. An oxcart carried the terra-cotta statue as far as a plantation west of Buenos Aires. But then, as the legend went, the oxen refused to move any farther until the statue of Mary was taken out of the cart.

As a result, this statue stayed near Buenos Aires, ending up in a shrine in the basilica of Luján. The statue was said to have performed many miracles. Centuries later, millions of pilgrims visit Luján every year.

In the years when Jorge was growing up, the Bergoglios went home from Sunday Mass to a leisurely midday Sunday dinner. There was always some kind of pasta, perhaps cappelletti (a hat-shaped pasta) with stew. Or maybe the potato dumplings called gnocchi, a favorite of Jorge's;

or maybe Piedmontese risotto, a rice dish. According to family lore, Regina had known nothing about preparing food when she married Mario, but Rosa Bergoglio had taught her to be an excellent cook.

The Bergoglios had to be very careful with their money—they couldn't afford to buy a car or take vacations. But they always had good food on the table. Likewise, the children always had decent clothes to wear. Regina was a clever seamstress, using the good fabric left in a worn-out shirt of Mario's, for instance, to make clothes for her sons and daughters.

Regina and Mario were a happy couple, in spite of so much hard work. He would often come home with flowers or other little presents for her. Together with their children, the grandparents, and many other relatives in Buenos Aires, they led a rich family life. Father Pozzoli was part of this circle too, and Jorge's Sivori grandparents would often invite the priest to dinner with the whole extended family.

On weekends Mario sometimes had to bring home extra work, bookkeeping ledgers to balance. However, he never complained about working so hard. He was a cheerful, even-tempered man who never punished his children physically, unusual in those times. Years later, Jorge's sister

María Elena would say that his personality reminded her of their father's.

While Mario pored over the ledgers, he lightened his work by listening to records of opera and popular Italian singers. The music filled the small house, to the enjoyment of all the Bergoglios. The family also entertained themselves on weekends by playing card games.

Mario, like most residents of Buenos Aires, was a soccer fan. He was intensely loyal to the underdog San Lorenzo team, founded by a Salesian missionary. He went to all the matches at the local stadium, and he took his family along. Jorge learned early to jump up and cheer when their team made a goal, and to shout names ("Good-for-nothing! Sellout!") at any referee who decided against San Lorenzo.

Regina Bergoglio's passion was for opera, and on Saturday afternoons she would gather the children around the family radio to listen to opera broadcasts. She explained the story of each opera—*Otello*, for instance—beforehand. As the opera went along, she reminded the children what was happening: "Listen up, now he [Otello] kills her." Although Jorge's mind sometimes drifted, these Saturday afternoon programs gave him a lifelong love of classical music.

• • •

Jorge started kindergarten in 1940 at the Sisters of Mercy Convent on the Avenida Directorio, a few blocks from home. The nuns noticed that he was a child with his own ideas, even at a young age. He loved to be outdoors, rather than in a classroom. And as Sister Maria Ilda remembered later, he "learned to do multiplications by going up and down the stairs. That was his method; the other children learned from a sheet of paper or by counting on their fingers."

The nuns were all fond of Jorge, a happy, affectionate boy. But he felt a special connection with one of the Sisters, Dolores Tortolo. She prepared Jorgito, "little George," for First Communion when he was eight years old.

Sister Dolores made sure that Jorge knew the catechism, the basic principles of the Catholic faith in question-and-answer form. She explained that Communion is the most important sacrament, or holy rite, in the Catholic Church. In Communion, Christians share bread, as Jesus Christ shared bread with his disciples at the Last Supper. Catholics believe that Christ is actually present in the Communion bread and wine.

Basics of the
Roman Catholic Faith

The Roman Catholic faith is summed up in the Nicene
Creed, dating from the fourth century:

I believe in one God,
the Father almighty,
maker of heaven and earth,
of all things visible and invisible.

I believe in one Lord Jesus Christ,
the Only Begotten Son of God,
born of the Father before all ages.
God from God, Light from Light,
true God from true God,
begotten, not made, consubstantial with the Father;
through him all things are made.
For us men and for our salvation
he came down from heaven,
and by the Holy Spirit was incarnate of the Virgin Mary,
and became man.
For our sake he was crucified under Pontius Pilate,
he suffered death and was buried,
and rose again on the third day
in accordance with the Scriptures.
He ascended into heaven
and is seated at the right hand of the Father.
He will come again in glory
to judge the living and the dead
and his kingdom will have no end.

I believe in the Holy Spirit, the Lord, the giver of life,
who proceeds from the Father and the Son,
who with the Father and the Son is adored and glorified,
who has spoken through the prophets.

I believe in one, holy, catholic and apostolic Church.
I confess one Baptism for the forgiveness of sins
and I look forward to the resurrection of the dead
and the life of the world to come. Amen.

This set of beliefs is usually recited during the Sunday
Mass before Communion.

These were all essential ideas for a young Catholic to learn.
But perhaps most important, Jorge absorbed from Sister
Dolores her attitude of hope and joy in the Christian life.

Before his First Communion, Jorge needed to make
his first confession of sin. Sister Dolores described how
he would do that, and what it meant. Kneeling in a confession box, he would tell a priest what he had done that
he shouldn't have done, and what he hadn't done that he
should have.

Jorge would promise to repent—he would say that he
was sorry, and that he would try not to commit those sins
again. Then the priest would say a prayer asking God's forgiveness, and give Jorge a penance, some action to help

cleanse the soul. The action might be some good work, and it would probably include saying prayers such as the Our Father or Hail Mary.

Jorge's grandmother had taught him, early on, that every human being commits sins, because they are imperfect. But God is always ready to forgive and help. Jorge knew that his father and his mother, his grandparents, and even especially good people, such as Father Pozzoli and Sister Dolores, went to confession to admit their sins and repent. Now he, too, would have a way to be sorry for his sins, to be forgiven, and to get help in becoming a better person.

On the day of his First Communion, in 1942, Jorge and the other children in his Communion class dressed in white. The girls wore white dresses, and Jorge wore a new white suit and white shoes. After the service, the Bergoglios celebrated with a big party.

In school, Jorge went on from the Sisters of Mercy Convent to Public School No. 8, the Cerviño School, five blocks from the Bergoglios' house. He adored his first-grade teacher, Estela Quiroga, and she loved Jorge. He was a polite and kind boy as well as a fast learner.

Jorge's classmates liked him too, and many of the boys were as eager to play soccer as he was.

From going to San Lorenzo soccer matches with his father, Jorge was an enthusiastic fan. After school, Jorge and the other boys ran to the nearby Herminia Brumana Square to play. In these neighborhood soccer games, Jorge wasn't a very good player, according to one friend, Hugo Morelli. But neither were any of the other boys.

But Jorge was different from his friends, in a way that they all noticed: he read for fun, and he read a lot. In his spare moments between school and family chores and playing soccer, Jorge always seemed to have his nose in a book.

Jorge's parents both enjoyed going to the movies, and they often took him along. There were always Italian movies playing in Buenos Aires, because of the large number of Italian immigrants. Two of the movies Jorge loved best were *La Strada* and *Rome, Open City*. *La Strada* is the tragic story of a brutish circus strongman and a simpleminded but loving young woman. In *Rome, Open City*, a courageous Italian woman dies trying to save her husband, a resistance fighter, from the Nazi occupiers.

• • •

In the background of Jorge Bergoglio's childhood, Argentina—and the world—were suffering through the Great Depression and then World War II. But Jorge was protected and nurtured by his strong, loving family, including his grandparents, uncles, aunts, and cousins, as well as his parents and brothers and sisters. The Catholic Church, which he knew through people like Father Pozzoli and Sister Dolores, was also strong and loving.

In many countries, including the United States, there is no established religion. But in Argentina, Roman Catholicism had been the official religion of the country since the nineteenth century. The government paid the bishops their salaries, and the president of Argentina could veto a bishop's appointment. In turn, the president had to be a baptized Catholic. The government in Argentina did not provide much in the way of social benefits to citizens who were unemployed or poor, and the Church was the main safety net for people who needed food, shelter, and medical help.

World War II broke out in Europe in 1939, when Jorge was almost three. Although Argentina did not join the combat on either side, the war caused hardship to the country.

The Argentinian economy depended on exports, but the war cut off all exports to the Nazi-occupied continent of Europe. Great Britain still welcomed goods from Argentina but refused to pay for them until the war was over.

The United States entered the fight against the Axis powers—Germany, Japan, and Italy—in 1941. In 1942 all the countries of Latin America followed suit—except Argentina. This was partly because of Argentina's unusual population, with a large of number of German immigrants. Also, many in the Argentinian upper classes and in the military were sympathetic to the Nazis. They believed the fascists were preventing the spread of communism.

The United States pressured Argentina to join the Allies, punishing the country by cutting off all trade. But Argentina remained stubbornly neutral until a few months before the war ended in 1945. Meanwhile, the people of Argentina steadily lost faith in the ruling political party, which kept itself in power through rigged elections. In 1943 the military—including a young officer named Juan Domingo Perón—seized control of the government.

When Jorge was nine, World War II ended. It was a day of great relief and excitement for Argentinians with European connections. For years, the many Italian immigrants in Buenos Aires had heard nothing from the relatives they'd left behind in Italy. The Bergoglios and their neighbors flocked to San José de Flores for a celebration Mass, and afterward neighbors shared news from across the Atlantic Ocean.

National elections were held once more in Argentina in 1946. At this time the Church supported Juan Perón. Peronism seemed to be an appealing third way in politics, between the atheistic communism of Soviet Russia and the fascism of Nazi Germany and Mussolini's Italy. Perón, already very popular, won the presidency by a landslide. He and his cabinet moved into the Casa Rosada, the pink mansion on the Plaza de Mayo that housed the national offices.

CHAPTER 3

THE DIGNITY
OF WORK

IN ARGENTINA, THE FIRST FEW YEARS AFTER WORLD
War II were hopeful for most citizens. Argentinians were
fiercely proud of their country, and President Perón
appealed to their pride. Argentina, Perón promised, did
not have to be dependent on Europe to buy its agricul-
tural exports, or on European companies to run its industries. Argentina could become a strong, self-sufficient
industrial nation. Perón's government took control of the
Central Bank of Argentina (heavily in debt to the Bank
of England), the railways (owned by British and French

companies), and the major exports of the country.

Perón also promised that the laborers of Argentina would finally get the better working conditions and better pay they deserved. Even before Perón's election in 1946, while he was secretary of labor, he had negotiated higher wages and better working conditions. Now that he was president, laws against school-age children working in factories and mines were passed. Workers gained many benefits, such as health care, paid vacations, and social security, and they could go out on strike without losing their jobs.

Just as important to laborers, President Perón gave them the respect they deserved. He was from a working-class family himself. Perón also had the support of much of the military. For them, he promised to modernize the armed forces and build up national security.

The Catholic Church approved of Perón's policies at first, because they were in tune with Catholic teaching on social justice. For many years, the Church had been concerned that the economic system of industrial capitalism ignored all the human beings it left unemployed, poor, and uneducated. At the same time, the Church was worried that communism, an antireligious ideology, appealed so strongly to the poor and the working classes. But Christianity itself contained a strong theme of social justice. (As Jorge Bergoglio would point out in later years, when he was a cardinal of the Church, this was the "great politics" of the Ten Commandments and the Gospels.)

Before World War II, Pope Pius XI had proposed a new, more humane capitalism in which industry owners and their employees worked in harmony. Under such a beneficial system, he explained, workers would not want to turn to communism. As president, Perón promised to bring the pope's vision to reality in Argentina. The Peronist government also provided many benefits for the Catholic Church, including increased salaries for bishops and funds to build seminaries, schools for training priests.

On top of being such a shrewd politician, Juan Perón was handsome and charming. And his wife, Eva, was a glamorous blond actress. Like Juan, Eva (fondly called "Evita") Perón was from a working-class background, and the people felt that this president and his wife understood them. Women loved Evita, and when women were given the right to vote in 1947, most of them supported the Peróns. President Perón was hugely popular during his first five-year term.

• • •

Meanwhile, the fifth and last child in the Bergoglio family, María Elena, was born in February 1948. The family was glad that she was a healthy baby, and that the family priest, Father Enrique Pozzoli, could baptize her. But Regina Bergoglio suffered complications from the birth. For months she was paralyzed, not even able to get out of bed.

The family decided that Grandmother Rosa would take care of the baby and the next youngest, Alberto, as she had cared for Jorge after Óscar was born. As for Jorge, Óscar, and Marta, Father Pozzoli helped to place them in boarding schools. The two boys went to Wilfrid Barón de los Santos Ángeles, a school run by the Salesian order in Ramos Mejía, a small city west of Buenos Aires.

Jorge spent only one year, the sixth grade, at Wilfrid Barón, but it was an important year. The Salesians organized the boys' days so that they had time for prayer, for quiet study, for sports, and for hobbies. Living in this peaceful setting, studying, and practicing the Catholic faith, all in an orderly routine, felt comfortable and right to twelve-year-old Jorge.

The priests at Wilfrid Barón also challenged the boys

to think about their faith in a more mature way. Listening to a priest tell about his own mother's death, Jorge realized for the first time that he also would die one day. But with confidence in the Catholic faith, he understood death as a natural part of life, and the thought did not frighten him.

Encouraged by his teachers, Jorge began to think about what he could do for other people. He was drawn to the idea of giving something up in order to help people who were truly needy. Along these lines, he began to wonder if he might become a priest when he grew up.

Jorge admired the priests he knew, especially Father Pozzoli. He prayed for guidance, and he discussed his future with one of the priests at Wilfrid Barón. But nothing more came of the idea at that time.

Jorge knew that if he became a priest, he would never marry—and he liked girls, although he was a little shy with them. When he was twelve, he had his first crush, on Amalia Damonte, a girl in his neighborhood. He wrote her a letter asking her to marry him, illustrated with a drawing of the white house with a red tile roof that he planned to buy for them. If she refused to marry him, Jorge told her, he would become a priest.

Unfortunately, Amalia's father got hold of the letter. Furious, he punished Amalia and ordered her to stop seeing Jorge.

At the end of the school year, when Jorge, Óscar, and Marta returned home from boarding school, Regina Bergoglio was recovering from her paralysis. But she still couldn't stand up to cook, so the older children took over at the stove. When they came home each afternoon, they would find their mother in a kitchen chair, peeling the potatoes. She had laid out the ingredients for them, and she gave them step-by-step instructions for making the meal. "Now put this in the pot and that in the pan," and so on.

And so the Bergoglio children learned to cook. Later in life, Jorge would make good use of his kitchen skills, preparing food for himself and others. (After Jorge was elected pope, his sister María Elena informed reporters that her brother made "fantastic stuffed calamari. It's his favorite dish.")

In 1950, at the age of thirteen, Jorge began studying at Technical Industrial School No. 12 in Buenos Aires, specializing in nutrition. He was working toward a diploma in applied chemistry. Jorge's friend Hugo Morelli was a classmate at this school as well.

Hugo remembered how obvious Jorge's unusual intelligence was, even in this group of bright boys. "He was always a step ahead of all of us." Jorge excelled in the subjects of literature, psychology, and religion, as well as chemistry. He seemed to understand immediately everything they were taught, but he didn't lord it over his fellow students. He was glad to help them with schoolwork.

Besides his extra-quick mind, Jorge stood out among the other boys for his love of reading. He read classic European authors such as Dostoevsky and Dante; he also read Argentinian literature. All his life, one of his favorites was *El Gaucho Martín Fierro*, a nineteenth-century epic poem by José Fernandez. This story is about the way of life of the gauchos, the cowboys of Argentina, and their role in gaining independence from Spain for their country.

Regina was proud of her oldest son's success at school. She hoped that he would go on to study at the university and become a doctor of medicine. In the 1950s in Argentina, medicine would be an unusual career for a boy from a lower-middle-class family like the Bergoglios. But Jorge was unusually bright, mature, and hardworking, and she was sure he would succeed.

Meanwhile, Mario judged that Jorge, at age thirteen,

was now old enough to begin earning money. He got his son a part-time job as a janitor at the hosiery factory where he was bookkeeper. So Jorge went to school from eight a.m. to one p.m., and then he worked from two p.m. to eight p.m.

At that time, President Perón was supporting the Church's mission to spread Christianity in Argentina. His government required religious education classes in the public schools, including Jorge's Technical Industrial School No. 12. Jorge told the teacher of his religious education class that he would be glad to help any of his classmates prepare for First Communion.

It turned out that two of the boys in the class, including Óscar Crespo, had not yet received First Communion, even though they were fourteen. Jorge coached them beforehand on the Church's teachings about the Eucharist and went with them to San José de Flores for the ceremony. And then Jorge brought them back to his house for a celebration lunch. In his zeal for the Catholic faith too, he was unusual among his classmates.

Between school and his part-time job, Jorge spent long hours working. But he didn't resent the responsibility; he was proud of his work. He knew that his family needed the money, and he knew how hard his parents worked. Throughout his life, he would believe that a person's work, no matter how humble, was necessary for their self-esteem. "Work anoints a person with dignity," he told interviewers when he was archbishop of Buenos Aires.

When Jorge was about sixteen, he joined the Catholic Action youth group in his local parish. It was a family tradition. Mario, his father, had been a member of Catholic Action when the family first moved to Buenos Aires, and Grandma Rosa had been a Catholic Action leader in her youth.

At San José de Flores, Jorge helped set up and run the bookshop at the church. He listened to the priests' talks on applying the teachings of the Church to social problems, especially poverty. He joined in visiting and helping the poorest people in the parish.

Fortunately, Jorge was energetic and didn't need much sleep. He had time for fun with his schoolmates, including Óscar Crespo and Hugo Morelli. Jorge's friends called him "El Flaco" (the thin one), and "baby face," because he looked so young.

A group of fifteen to twenty of Jorge's friends got

together for parties at one another's homes; they went on picnics at the Costanera Sur resort on the La Plata River. They played pool at a neighborhood bar; they dressed up in suits and went dancing at nightclubs. Jorge loved tango music, especially the songs of Ada Falcón.

Jorge was a little shy, but he was a good tango dancer. Anna Colonna, a friend from the parish of San José de Flores, remembered later how politely he would ask a girl to be his partner for a dance. His favorite dance was the *milonga*, similar to the tango but faster.

After three years of studying chemistry, Jorge was able to get a better part-time job. He left the hosiery factory and started working in a food laboratory, evaluating the chemicals in nutrients. He was deeply impressed by his boss, a Paraguayan woman named Esther Ballestrino de Careaga. She expected all the work to be done to the highest standards. If he did a job suspiciously quickly, she would ask him if he'd actually tested the substance. "What for?" Jorge asked. "If I've done all the previous tests, it would surely be more or less the same."

His boss would not accept such sloppiness. "No, you have to do things properly." In her laboratory, Jorge said later, he learned to take work seriously. She also reinforced his father's work ethic: that a job well done, no matter how lowly, earns dignity for the worker.

Esther de Careaga had been exiled from Paraguay for her communist sympathies, and Jorge was intrigued by her political views. She encouraged Jorge to read Communist Party literature, and he discussed it with her and with his friends. A teacher at his high school was also a communist, and he, too, talked to the students about politics. Jorge enjoyed the free exchange of political ideas. But he could not accept the atheism—the rejection of belief in God—that was part of communist ideology.

Hugo Morelli and Jorge had vigorous arguments over politics. Hugo was a firm supporter of President Juan Perón. Jorge agreed with the Peronist goal of social justice, but he was disturbed by Perón's increasing conflict with the Catholic Church. But they could both laugh at the Peronist parrot living next door to their school. The bird would interrupt class sessions with its piercing screech: *¡Viva Perón, carajo!* (Long live Perón, damn it!)

Perón's policies had resulted in prosperity for the first few years. But by the early 1950s, Argentina was suffering from runaway inflation. Prices rose and rose, and so did unemployment. Increasingly, Perón ruled more as a dictator than as the leader of a democracy.

By 1951, Perón and the Church were in conflict. One sore point between them was that for many years, the government of Argentina had had the right to appoint the bishops, the Catholic leaders. The Church wanted to be free of such government control, but Perón wanted to appoint bishops who would support him politically.

Perón began a campaign to convince the people of Argentina that he, not the Church, was the one with the Christian values. His wife, Eva, wrote in her autobiography, "Perón is the face of God in the darkness." Evita was beloved by working-class people, especially women. She established a foundation to provide badly needed orphanages, medical clinics, and nursing homes, and spent hours of her personal time with sick and needy people. Perón was reelected toward the end of 1951 by a wide margin, in spite of the struggling economy and a severe drought.

Shortly before Eva's death from cancer in July 1952, Perón appointed her to the official position of Spiritual Leader of the Nation. Catholic leaders were outraged, but indeed Evita was a saint for the poor in the minds of thousands of Argentinians. Perón encouraged the idea with a picture in the school edition of her autobiography, showing Evita with a halo like the Virgin Mary's.

Meanwhile, in Jorge's busy young life, along with family and school, work and friends, he felt a growing sense of direction. From his early childhood he had looked up to Father Pozzoli, the Bergoglios' family priest. Father Pozzoli was a close friend as well as protector and spiritual director, and Jorge admired him as an ideal of what a parish priest should be. Also, in Jorge's year of boarding school, he had experienced what a life dedicated to the Church might be like.

Then one day in September, when Jorge Bergoglio was almost seventeen, he heard an unmistakable call.

CHAPTER 4
THE CALL

ON A SPRING MORNING IN SEPTEMBER 1953, JORGE Bergoglio set out to meet his friends. It was the beginning of the season in the Southern Hemisphere, and the jacaranda trees around Buenos Aires were draped with clusters of purple-blue blossoms. This special day, September 21, was National Students' Day in Argentina.

Jorge headed down the Avenida Rivadavia toward the Flores station, where he intended to catch a train to Technical Industrial School No. 12. He was looking forward to a day of fun, to the students' picnic outing, and to spending time with one special girl. According to an interview with his sister María Elena years later, her brother was going to propose marriage to his girlfriend that day.

But on the way to the station, Jorge paused outside his church, San José de Flores. Impulsively he turned aside and entered the church, just for a moment, to say a prayer. Inside, he noticed a priest he had never seen before.

There was something special about this man, a deeply spiritual quality. Jorge watched the priest sit down in one of the confessional booths, ready to listen through the wooden screen. Jorge "felt like someone grabbed me from inside and took me to the confessional."

Kneeling in the booth, making his confession, Jorge had the overwhelming sense that he was meeting someone, "someone who had been waiting for me for a long time." He felt that this someone was looking at him with great understanding and love. It was as if God was saying to him, "I ask for you by name, I choose you, and the only thing I ask is that you let yourself be loved." From that moment, Jorge was sure that he was meant to become a priest.

Jorge was overwhelmed. Instead of continuing on to the Students' Day celebration, he returned home. He pondered what had happened. God had sprung a surprise on him.

Jorge had thought that in choosing to make his confession that day, he was seeking God. But he discovered that God was already with him, looking on him with mercy and choosing him. God knew him better than he knew himself. "From that moment on," he said later, "God is the One who *te primerea*—'springs it on you.'"

For Jorge Bergoglio, closeness to God would always have this element of surprise. "If the religious experience doesn't have this measure of astonishment, of surprise, if this compassion is not sprung upon you—then it's cold, it doesn't draw us in completely," he told interviewers later. His experience on Students' Day also set his standard for what confession was meant to be—not, as Pope Francis would say, "like taking your clothes to the dry cleaner."

Coincidentally—or maybe not—that same day, September 21, was the feast day of Saint Matthew. In the Gospel story, Matthew was an unlikely candidate for sainthood. He was one of those despicable people who served the Roman occupiers by wringing taxes (plus a surcharge for himself) from the people of Palestine. Knowing this, Jesus surprised Matthew in his tax office and said, "Follow me."

At this time, in September 1953, Jorge didn't tell his family of his decision. But he did confide in his friend Óscar Crespo. "I'm going to finish secondary school with you guys, but I'm not going to be a chemist. I'm going to be a priest." He began spiritual direction under the priest he had met that day in the church, Father Duarte Ibarra, until Father Ibarra died the following year.

As he had planned, Jorge graduated from the technical school in 1955, earning a diploma as a chemical technician. And then he applied to the Inmaculada Concepción Seminary, where parish priests for the diocese of Buenos Aires were trained. He was accepted and scheduled to enter the seminary in March 1956.

Meanwhile, Jorge continued to study. He let his mother think that he planned to become a doctor, as she hoped. Regina cleared a space in the attic, away from the noisy family, for him to study medicine. She thought he was set on this course—until the day she went to clean his special room. Instead of medical textbooks, she discovered he was reading books on theology.

Regina realized that he must be seriously considering going into a seminary, and she was very angry. When Jorge came home, she confronted him with his lie. He pretended he hadn't deceived her. "I *am* studying medicine—but medicine of the soul." His mother didn't think that reply was clever, funny, or an acceptable explanation.

Jorge finally told his father, all joking aside, that he had decided to become a priest. Mario Bergoglio, as a devout man, was happy for his son. He broke the news to his wife, who still did not accept it. She urged Jorge to earn a university degree first before he made up his mind. Mario agreed with Regina that it would be wise for Jorge to try the university, but Jorge's mind was already made up.

However, Jorge did go to see Father Pozzoli to discuss his decision. Jorge told him about his sense of being called, which hadn't changed since that day in September 1953, and about his parents' objections. Father Pozzoli gave Jorge his blessing; as for the disagreement with his parents, he told Jorge to leave it to God.

Since Father Pozzoli had been the Bergoglios' friend and guide for so many years, they were open to listening to his views. But, as Jorge noticed admiringly, Pozzoli did not try to tell them what to do. He waited to bring up the subject at a pleasant social occasion, when he and the family were having breakfast after a special Mass.

Father Pozzoli began by agreeing with Regina and Mario that university study might be a good idea for Jorge. Then he told stories about how people he knew had decided to enter the priesthood. He told them about his own calling.

Jorge saw that Father Pozzoli was "softening up" his father and mother so that they would come to the right conclusion on their own. "When he sensed that he was getting what he wanted, he pulled back before anyone else realized." But Jorge did realize what the priest was doing, and he saw how well his method worked.

In contrast, Grandmother Rosa did not have to be persuaded or "softened." When Jorge told her of his calling, she was not even surprised. "Well, if God has called you," she said, "blessed be."

Jorge's circle of friends were glad for him, because he was so clearly sure and happy that he was called to be a priest. At the same time, they were sorry to see him leave. The boys who'd played billiards and soccer with Jorge teased him that the San Lorenzo soccer team was losing a great player. Some of the girls who'd danced the tango with him shed tears. They would all miss him.

By this time, Jorge had considered the weighty decision for years. He knew that in taking the vows to become a Catholic priest, he would have to promise to remain celibate. That meant that he would never marry, and he would never have children.

This would not be an easy sacrifice. Jorge enjoyed the company of girls and women, and he had had a serious girlfriend during his secondary school days. From his own happy childhood, Jorge knew how delightful and satisfying family life could be. But as a priest, he would be free from the complications of marriage and family—free to love and serve people wherever God led him. He was certain that this was God's will for him, and also his own deepest desire.

In March 1956 Jorge Bergoglio began his preparation for the priesthood at the Inmaculada Concepción Seminary in Buenos Aires. His mother, still badly disappointed, refused to go to see him off that day. The seminary was a massive gray building with iron bars on the windows, taking up a whole block in the Villa Devoto neighborhood. The school was run by priests of the Society of Jesus, or Jesuits, an order of teachers and missionaries.

Parishes and Orders

The basic organization in the Catholic Church is the local parish, usually one church congregation. A priest, the pastor, is responsible for the parish. A group of parishes in one area, called a diocese, is presided over by a bishop. An archbishop, such as the archbishop of Buenos Aires, oversees a collection of dioceses, or an archdiocese. And archbishops are under the authority of the pope, the head of the worldwide Catholic Church.

But another important set of organizations within the Church is the religious institutes. These organizations include orders: sisters, such as the Sisters of Mercy, and priests or monks, such as the Franciscans or the Jesuits. Each order has its own special purpose. Some orders live in monasteries and convents in seclusion from the world. Other orders, like the Jesuits, interact with the world—for instance, as teachers, missionaries, or nurses.

To become established in the Church, an order must be approved by the pope, and the pope is the ultimate authority over each order.

The students' life in the seminary was highly organized. The day began early with the morning prayer service in the chapel and was punctuated with noonday Mass, the evening prayer service, and again prayers before bedtime. In between, the boys ate meals together in silence, and they studied.

Many of the boys in the seminary came from expensive private schools, where they had already learned to read Latin and Greek. But Jorge had not, so his studies included those languages, which he would need for studying philosophy and theology. The boys were given free time for sports such as soccer, which Jorge still played with zest, and still with not much talent. The other students nicknamed him "El Gringo" (the foreigner), probably because he looked more Italian than Latin American.

Jorge was one of the older students, and he was especially mature and serious. He was made a prefect, a student leader. Among other duties, the prefect rang the bell in the morning to awaken the other students. One of Jorge's younger charges at the seminary was Leonardo Sandri, who would later rise to an important position in the Vatican. Leonardo admired his prefect as an ideal priest-in-training: Jorge was devout and enthusiastic about his calling, but he also had a sense of humor.

There was a dog living at the seminary, and Jorge loved that animal. However, he knew he couldn't have a pet, any more than he could get married and have a family. A priest had to be unattached, except to God's will.

During his time in the seminary, Jorge went through a

moment of rethinking his desire to become a priest. Even his Grandmother Rosa, who was so proud of and happy at his calling, had reminded him that he could change his mind at any time before he took his vows. "Please never forget that the doors to this house are always open," she told him, "and no one will reproach you for anything if you decide to come back."

At the wedding of an uncle, Jorge met one young woman in particular who lingered in his mind. Back in the seminary, he kept thinking about this young woman, especially when he tried to pray. She was beautiful, she was intelligent, and he was very taken with her.

If Jorge was so attracted to a woman, did that mean he was mistaken about his vocation? For a whole week, Jorge struggled to find the serenity in prayer that meant so much to him. But finally his devotion to his calling won out.

While Jorge Bergoglio was working out his path in life, Argentina was going through one of its many political upheavals. Juan Perón, president since 1946, was furious with the Catholic Church. He was governing according to the Church's social values, and he was giving the Church many benefits. Therefore, he assumed, they should let him use the Church to control the people. But the Argentine bishops' first loyalty was to the pope in Rome.

To punish the Church for resisting him, Perón cut off money for Catholic schools and outlawed Catholic Action. He began to arrest priests and close churches. He outlawed public religious acts, such as the popular processions on Catholic holy days.

During 1955 Catholics organized to defy these anti-Catholic laws, staging processions so huge that Perón could not enforce his law against them. In June, on the Catholic feast day of Corpus Christi, a crowd of 250,000, including university students and middle-class people, marched through downtown Buenos Aires. Perón, unnerved, arrested a number of priests and raided Catholic Action offices.

By this time, a large faction of the military had also turned against Perón. When Peronist union members gathered for a counterdemonstration in the Plaza de Mayo, Buenos Aires' main square, officers at the naval air force sent warplanes to fly over them. The planes, armed with bombs and machine guns, were painted with the slogan "*Cristo Vence*" (Christ Conquers). They killed over a hundred Peronist demonstrators. Jorge Bergoglio, as a devout

Catholic, was sickened by the slaughter of innocent people in the name of Jesus Christ.

And it was the Christians, not the military, whom Peronists attacked in revenge, burning down twelve churches. Perón stepped up his propaganda campaign against the Catholic Church. The anti-Perón military plotted to overthrow him. In September 1955, they finally succeeded, and Perón fled the country.

But the coup, the military takeover, did not bring peace and stability to Argentina either. The first head of the military government was quickly replaced by General Pedro Aramburu. The next year, 1956, when Jorge entered the seminary, a cousin of his took part in an uprising against Aramburu. The rebellion failed, and Jorge's cousin, Lieutenant Colonel Óscar Lorenzo Cogorno, was executed by a firing squad. During the following ten years, one government after another tried to keep order, but the bitter divisions in the country only grew.

CHAPTER 5

"YOU ARE IMITATING CHRIST"

AS JORGE BERGOGLIO STUDIED AND PRAYED AND played soccer, he thought about what kind of priest he wanted to become. The purpose of the Buenos Aires seminary was to train young men to become parish priests. A parish priest was one assigned to oversee a particular church, such as Jorge's childhood church, San José. However, there were other possible kinds of work for Catholic priests. For instance, members of the Society of Jesus, the Jesuit order, were not parish priests, but teachers or missionaries. The rector, the head of the seminary, was a priest belonging to the Society of Jesus. So was Jorge's spiritual director, and so were many of the teachers.

More and more, the Jesuits attracted Jorge. Jesuits had the reputation of being especially tough, smart, and dedicated. Their inspiring Latin motto was *Ad maiorem Dei gloriam,* "For the greater glory of God."

The Society of Jesus (Jesuits)

The founder of the Society of Jesus was a sixteenth-century Spaniard, Ignatius Loyola. Trained as a courtier and soldier, he wore the latest fashions, romanced the ladies, and picked deadly fights with anyone who offended him. His only goal was to gain glory for himself.

Then at age thirty, in a battle between the Spanish and the French, Ignatius was hit in the leg by a cannonball. He had to spend several months recovering, with nothing to do except read and think. And the only available books were about the life of Jesus Christ and the lives of the saints.

To his surprise, Ignatius was fascinated by the story of a thirteenth-century saint, Francis of Assisi, a man like himself from a wealthy family. Francis had rejected his riches and social position and chosen a life of poverty, inspiring many followers. Ignatius began to ask himself, What if *I* gave up my wealth and noble rank? How would *I* follow Jesus?

After years of traveling, studying, and contemplation, Ignatius decided that he was not meant to serve God in a monastery. Instead, he would go out into the world to convert nonbelievers to Christianity. With only a few followers, he founded a new order, the Society of Jesus. It was approved by Pope Paul III in 1540.

The Jesuit missionaries set out immediately to spread the Gospel in Asia and the newly discovered Americas, often to people who had never heard of Jesus Christ. Many of the missionaries died in their dangerous work, but more and more joined the order.

During the seventeenth century, in South America, Jesuits converted many thousands of the indigenous Guarani people to Christianity. The missionaries organized the Guarani into "reductions" or villages. These communities developed thriving industries, such as the production of the tea called maté. They protected themselves from the Spanish and Portuguese colonists who wanted to enslave them.

But early in the eighteenth century, the Jesuit order was dissolved by the pope, and the missionaries were expelled from South America. They were not allowed to return to Argentina until the mid–nineteenth century. From then on, the Jesuits in Argentina concentrated on education—founding and running excellent schools and universities.

To Jorge Bergoglio, the life of Saint Ignatius Loyola, declared a saint by Pope Gregory XV in 1622, was as inspiring as the life of Saint Francis had been to Ignatius. Jorge was also inspired by stories of the heroic Jesuit missionaries who had worked in South America during the colonial period. He was not discouraged by the Jesuits' high standards, or by their emphasis on discipline and obedience. In fact, he sensed that discipline and obedience was just what he needed.

In order to become a Jesuit priest, Jorge would have to undergo thirteen years of rigorous training, including earning a university degree. And he would have to give up any ambitions of a glorious career, because a Jesuit had to promise not to seek higher office in the Church. For that reason, there had never been a Jesuit pope.

To Jorge, all the challenges of the Jesuit life were attractions. He was eager to serve God as a missionary. Jorge didn't want to be a priest who waited in a church for people to come to him. He wanted to go out—even to the other side of the world—to find the people who needed him.

In August 1957, the year after he entered the Buenos Aires seminary, Jorge was stricken with a life-threatening fever. He was choking with pleurisy, an inflammation of the lining of the chest cavity. Antibiotics did not seem to help. By the time he was taken to the hospital, he could hardly breathe.

The doctors discovered that Jorge had pneumonia, caused by cysts on his right lung. Part of that lung had to be removed, along with the cysts. During the surgery, two of his fellow seminary students donated blood for him, in the person-to-person transfusion that was used at that time. Afterward, Jorge spent several days in an oxygen tent to help his breathing.

To clean Jorge's chest cavity, tubes were put in to flush it out with saline solution and drain it. This treatment was necessary to save his life, but it caused him terrible and constant pain. He had never in his young life suffered so much, and the ordeal continued for weeks.

At one point, delirious, Jorge clutched his mother and begged, "Tell me, what's happening to me?" Regina tried to encourage him with cheerful words, and so did other visitors. But cheerful words, when he was in agony and in danger of dying, did not help him.

Only Dolores Tortolo, the same Sister of Mercy who had prepared Jorge for First Communion years ago, offered a way for Jorge to make sense of his torment. She told him, "With your pain, you are imitating Christ."

Sister Dolores meant that Jorge's suffering was a kind of participation in the lonely agony that Jesus suffered on the cross. The idea gave Jorge peace. As he explained later, "Pain is not a virtue in itself, but you can be virtuous in the way you bear it."

Given this insight, Jorge felt strengthened in his faith. Perhaps, also, he felt a closer connection with Saint Ignatius Loyola. Ignatius had been converted during his own convalescence from an agonizing wound and treatment.

Meanwhile, one of the nurses at the hospital decided that the reason the antibiotics were not working was that Jorge had not been given enough. She took the responsibility to triple his doses, and he began to improve. He grew strong enough to talk to another visitor, Father Pozzoli, about how he would follow his calling. The priest gave his blessing to Jorge's idea of joining the Jesuits.

In November 1957 Jorge took his first step on the long road to becoming a Jesuit priest. He applied to the Society of Jesus and was accepted for the following March. For the months in between, Father Pozzoli arranged for Jorge to spend the Southern Hemisphere summer at a Salesian retreat house, the Villa Don Bosco. The retreat house was in the hill country of Tandil, a more peaceful place than Buenos Aires for Jorge to finish recovering.

• • •

On March 11, 1958, Jorge Bergoglio began his novitiate at the Jesuit center in Córdoba, in north-central Argentina. The city of Córdoba had been founded by Jesuit missionaries in 1573, and its university, also founded by Jesuits in 1613, was the oldest in South America. The deep history of the Jesuit order was in the very buildings—the church, the priests' quarters, the university, the seminary—dating back to the seventeenth century.

The Society of Jesus is sometimes nicknamed "God's marines." Ignatius Loyola had been a soldier himself, and his order was run in a military manner. For Jorge Bergoglio and the other twenty-five novices at Córdoba, daily life was highly regulated. Jorge was used to an organized routine at the seminary in Buenos Aires, but the Jesuits required an even higher level of discipline.

The Jesuit Novitiate

In the first two years of Jesuit formation, the novices underwent discipline as strict, in its way, as that of marine recruits. They had no free time to socialize. Outside of classes and meals and sleep, a novice went from prayer to meditation to spiritual reading. Three times a day, for about fifteen minutes, he was expected to examine his conscience. That meant reflecting prayerfully on the last few hours, making himself aware of God's presence in his life.

The novitiate included six special month-long sessions. In one session, a retreat, the novices spent the entire month in silence, working through Ignatius's Spiritual Exercises. The Exercises began with contemplation of God's loving mercy. In guided meditation on scenes from scripture, the novices were urged to imagine themselves in each scene—for instance, at the foot of the cross during Jesus's crucifixion.

The Exercises also taught the skills of discernment, how to search for spiritual guidance. Paying attention to his own thoughts and feelings, the novice learned to judge whether they came from a good source or an evil one.

Two other month-long sessions reinforced the idea of a life of service. In one, the novices worked in hospitals with the sick and dying, performing lowly tasks such as emptying bedpans. In another, they performed humble chores around the Jesuit residence.

During a session known as pilgrimage, the novices were sent out to areas where they knew no one. They had to live by asking strangers for food and shelter, and they gained experience in poverty and humility. Other special sessions were spent teaching children in local schools, and practicing public speaking.

At the end of the two years, if the novice still believed that he was called to the Jesuit way of life, he took his first vows.

In frequent examinations of conscience, Jorge was taught to begin by looking for instances of God's presence in his life. He would remind himself of all the blessings he had to be grateful for. He would note a "consolation," a moment in which he had felt close to God, and another moment, a "desolation," in which he had felt distant from God. Praying about the desolation, he would try to understand how God was present, even in the moments when he felt distant.

Besides the thrice-daily private examinations, the novices were given chances to become aware of faults in themselves that they might not have noticed. From time to time, the novice master would choose one novice to be criticized by the others. Once, when it was Jorge's turn, his fellow students commented on the irritating "pious long faces" he made when taking Communion or walking in the corridor.

The novices in Córdoba had no free time to socialize. In fact, they were discouraged from forming close friendships. This was practice for their future lives as Jesuits, when they might be sent on mission far away from everyone they knew. Jorge's friend Goma, from the parish of San José de Flores, was also one of the novices, but these old pals were required to call each other "Brother Bergoglio" and "Brother Manent." (However, according to what his sister María Elena said later, Jorge did make friends with a parakeet at the Jesuit center and taught it some words.)

Throughout these two years, the novices were trained not to care about social standing, or money, or power. Like Jesus, they should be equally at ease at a rich man's banquet or sharing a piece of bread with a beggar. Like Jesus, they should be willing to get down on their knees and wash dirty feet.

For Jorge, who had been brought up to pitch in and do whatever work needed doing, it was nothing out of the ordinary to wash clothes, sweep floors, and wait on tables. But for many of the novices from upper-class families, these would have been new and humiliating experiences.

Jorge was excused from the pilgrimage session, probably to his disappointment. Although he had recovered from his ordeal with pneumonia, he had a tendency to shortness of breath. His health would never again be quite as strong as before his illness. But he had more time for reading. Two books on his shelf that he returned to again and again were a biography of Saint Francis of Assisi and Saint Thérèse of Lisieux's *Story of a Soul*.

During the second year of Jorge's novitiate, the Jesuits-in-training at Córdoba had an exciting visitor. He was Father Pedro Arrupe, head of the Jesuit missionaries in Japan. Arrupe told the novices thrilling stories about the first Jesuit missionaries to East Asia, including Francis Xavier, Matteo Ricci, and Roberto de Nobili.

Arrupe also showed the novices a documentary film of the bombing of Hiroshima on August 6, 1945. He himself had been teaching novices on the island at the time of the event. He saw the blinding light as the first atom bomb exploded above the city, consuming it with fire. Arrupe tended to the victims, among them many of the thousands who died.

Jorge and Goma were so inspired by Father Arrupe that they each asked him to accept them for the mission in Japan. But Arrupe answered that they would not be ready for such an assignment for several years, after they had studied philosophy and theology. Then they could apply to the Jesuit superior general in Rome, head of the worldwide Society of Jesus.

• • •

The overarching purpose of the two-year novitiate was to help each young man decide whether or not he was truly called to the life of a Jesuit. For Jorge Bergoglio, the answer was yes. On March 12, 1960, he took his vows of poverty, chastity, and obedience. Although he would not be an ordained priest for many more years, he was now a member of the Society of Jesus. He had the right to sign his name *Jorge Bergoglio, SJ.*

CHAPTER 6

WINDS
OF CHANGE

IT WAS THE FALL OF 1960 IN THE SOUTHERN HEMI-
sphere when Jorge Bergoglio and his friend Goma
Manent climbed into a truck and left Córdoba. They
were heading west to enter the second stage of their
formation as Jesuits. This stage, called the "juniorate,"
would take place in Chile, on the western side of the
Andes Mountains. The juniors from the whole southern
cone of South America—Chile, Argentina, Uruguay,
Paraguay, and Bolivia—were trained there.

The truck carried the juniors from Córdoba as far

as the city of Mendoza, at the foot of the Andes. From Mendoza they flew over the mountains to Santiago, Chile. They would spend their next year at the Casa Loyola, the Jesuit formation house.

The Casa Loyola was out in the countryside, with vegetable gardens, apple and pear orchards, and farm animals. During the week, the students spent most of their waking time in classes, from nine a.m. to one p.m., and from two thirty in the afternoon to eight in the evening. They studied Latin, Greek, literature, oratory, rhetoric, art, and culture.

As at Córdoba, the students ate meals in silence, listening to a reading or to a student giving a practice talk. They did not have radios or newspapers. They did have an afternoon break for tea, when they were allowed to chat—although they were supposed to speak to each other in Latin, the official language of the Roman Catholic Church.

Jorge was especially quiet and studious, but the other juniors found him interesting to talk with. The students sometimes discussed their futures, and Jorge had definite ideas about what he wanted to do. He wanted to be a Jesuit in charge of the formation, or training, of future Jesuits.

Even though the juniors at Santiago were shut off from

the outside world, they were aware of the ongoing political struggles in South America. At that time, the politics of Latin American countries were strongly influenced by the Cold War rivalry between the United States and Soviet Russia. The United States was alarmed by Fidel Castro's communist revolution in Cuba, only ninety-three miles from the tip of Florida. In Washington, they feared that similar revolutions would succeed throughout Latin America. Many in the U.S. government had regarded Juan Perón's socialism in Argentina as dangerously close to Soviet communism.

Since the military coup overthrowing Perón in 1955, the Peronist party in Argentina had not been allowed to take part in elections. Some of Jorge's fellow students, especially those from the upper classes, felt that this policy was necessary. But Jorge thought it was wrong, although he had disagreed with President Perón's actions against the Catholic Church.

The schedule for the juniors at Casa Loyola was a little more relaxed than for the novices at Córdoba, with time twice a week for the students to play volleyball and basketball. Unfortunately, Jorge, because of his damaged right lung, could not play team sports or join in the weekend camping trips. But he did get some exercise by swimming.

On weekends, the juniors put on black cassocks—full-length, close-fitting robes—and went out on missions from the Casa Loyola to the neighboring village of Marruecos. The villagers were poor tenant farmers. Jorge had seen many poor people in Buenos Aires, and he had helped bring food to needy families in his own parish. But he and the other students were shocked at the extreme poverty of the villagers.

These families lived in shacks with tin roofs and without proper sanitation. Often they had nothing to eat. The children came to the little school where Jorge taught religion, dirty and without shoes, even in the bitterest cold.

His heart was touched by an old woman in the village who begged him, "*Padrecito* ["little priest," although Jorge and the other juniors were not yet priests], if I could get hold of a blanket, how good that would be, *padrecito*."

Teaching children the Catholic faith was not an easy assignment. As Father Jorge Bergoglio would say later, someone who is able to make the catechism simple enough for a child to understand is a wise person. That was especially true of the children of Marruecos, whose families were not bringing them up in the Christian faith. He wrote his eleven-year-old sister, María Elena, "The worst of it is that they don't know Jesus." Evidently, he didn't need to go to Japan to find people to convert to Christianity.

Jorge asked María Elena to help him by praying the rosary every night for his mission to these children. Of all his brothers and sisters, Jorge had a special bond with María Elena. She was the "little doll" of the family, and he was "El Viejo" (the old man), as she called him. He looked after her, almost like a second father.

For Jorge Bergoglio's next stage in his Jesuit training, he returned to Argentina. In March 1961 he began two years of studying philosophy at the Colegio Máximo de San José. The Colegio Máximo was a stately redbrick building on a 120-acre estate in San Miguel, about sixty miles from the city of Buenos Aires. This intellectual center had been founded for training Jesuits, and it was run by the Jesuits, but students from other Catholic orders also studied there. In fact, scholars came from all over South America to do research at the Colegio's excellent library.

At the Colegio Máximo, Jorge made good use of his expertise in the kitchen, which he'd learned during the year when his mother was recovering from paralysis. On

Sundays, the cook's day off, he prepared meals for the other students. Interviewers asked him years later whether he was a good cook. "No one ever died," he answered.

As for the course work, Jorge thought most of the philosophy they read was too dry. Goma, who had progressed with him to the Colegio Máximo, agreed. The reading they were assigned was intellectually sophisticated, but it was removed from the real joys and suffering of real people. And after all, they had become Jesuits in order to serve people. Jorge Bergoglio later criticized this kind of philosophy as useless, because "it loses sight of the human or even . . . is afraid of the human, or deluded about itself."

One philosophy professor who did inspire Jorge was Miguel Fiorito, who also became his spiritual adviser. Fiorito had a deep understanding of Saint Ignatius Loyola's approach to spiritual discernment, and Jorge learned a great deal from him. Throughout Jorge's life, he would depend on discernment in prayer in making decisions, large or small.

The same year that Jorge began his studies at the Colegio Máximo, he was shaken by a personal loss. Father Enrique

Pozzoli, the Bergoglios' dear friend and spiritual guide ever since their arrival in Buenos Aires, fell very ill and was taken to the hospital. He was elderly, and it was clear that he did not have long to live. Jorge went to the hospital, intending to visit his old friend one last time. But instead, at the moment when he was called into Father Pozzoli's room, Jorge left the hospital. The priest died soon afterward. Jorge never understood why he had avoided saying good-bye to Pozzoli, and he always regretted it.

Perhaps he had been overwhelmed by losing his spiritual father, as well as his actual father. Before Pozzoli's death, Mario Bergoglio had died in the San Lorenzo soccer stadium of a sudden heart attack. Jorge's youngest brother, Alberto, was with Mario Bergoglio at that soccer game, and he was so devastated that he never went to the stadium again.

In contrast to the lifeless philosophy that Jorge had to study at the Colegio Máximo, there were exciting signs of growth and renewal in the worldwide Catholic Church. The year 1962 marked a milestone in its history: Pope John XXIII, elected in 1958, called the Second Vatican Council.

Jorge and Goma were both impressed by Pope John XXIII. He was from a family of Italian sharecroppers in Lombardy, one of fourteen children. Unlike the aristocratic Pope Pius XII before him, he was a warm, down-to-earth man, and he was passionate about peace. In October 1962, the same month that he opened the Second Vatican Council, John XXIII offered to mediate between U.S. president John Kennedy and Soviet premier Nikita Khrushchev in the Cuban Missile Crisis. Both sides praised the pope, although they did not accept his offer.

The Second Vatican Council

Pope John XXIII called the Second Vatican Council, also known as Vatican II, in 1962. The purpose of this gathering was to decide how the Catholic Church should relate to the modern world. Therefore, the council brought to Rome bishops from all over the globe, as well as theologians, laypeople, and observers from the Protestant denominations and the Eastern branches of the Catholic Church.

A worldwide council of the Catholic Church was an unusual event. The First Vatican Council, interrupted by the war of Italian unification, had been convened almost a century before. Previous to that, the last such council was the Council of Trent, in the sixteenth century.

Many cardinals and archbishops, including some from Argentina, thought there was no need for a council in 1962. Church policy, in their view, should be made from the top—the pope and his advisers—down. But John XXIII was committed to increasing equality in the Church. "We were all made in God's image, and thus, we are all Godly alike," he declared.

Pope John XXIII died in 1963, but Vatican II continued under his successor, Paul VI, and ended in December 1965. In the authoritative teachings that resulted, the council urged a more open Church, one more engaged with the lives of real human beings—especially the poor. The council recommended translating the liturgy from Latin to local languages, involving laypeople in worship services, and adding more reading of scripture. The council advised that the pope share decision-making with the bishops. Furthermore, the council advised reconciliation with other Christian denominations, as well as friendship with Jews and Muslims.

The effects of these recommendations were far-reaching, and Catholics continue to interpret them in different ways and to debate whether the Second Vatican Council was helpful or harmful to the Church.

Jorge and Goma followed closely the progress of Vatican II, as the council was called. They posted notices about every development on a bulletin board in the Colegio

Máximo. The questions the Second Vatican Council was considering seemed like an answer to Jorge's dissatisfaction with his philosophy courses. The council aimed to reconnect the Church to the modern world in order to carry out its very reason for being: spreading Christianity. This sounded more like the missionary zeal, expressed by Ignatius Loyola's "Go forth and set the world on fire," that had first attracted Jorge Bergoglio to the Society of Jesus.

Another friend of Jorge's who hoped for Vatican II to reform the Church was Fernando Montes, a student at the Colegio Máximo from Chile. Jorge and Fernando had many long discussions as they watched the other students play soccer. Jorge couldn't play because of his damaged lung, and Fernando would rather talk than kick a soccer ball. So they stood on the sidelines, sipping gourds of the smoky tea called maté and talking about Vatican II.

Jorge Bergoglio and his friends, along with many younger people, looked forward to the reforms of Vatican II. However, other Catholics, including some of the bishops in Argentina, were horrified at the thought of changing the Church in any way. They were determined to resist.

• • •

In the meantime, Jorge Bergoglio finished his philosophy studies in 1963 with the final examination, a grueling test. It was an oral exam, conducted in Latin, facing a panel of ten Jesuits. But he passed with high marks.

Jorge immediately wrote to Rome, as Father Pedro Arrupe had advised him back in 1959, asking again to be sent to Japan as a missionary. Father Arrupe himself had recently been elected superior general, the world head of the Society of Jesus. He judged that the eager young Jesuit was not physically strong enough, because of his damaged lung, to serve as a missionary, so he refused Jorge's request.

Arrupe's letter was kind, but this was a deep disappointment to Jorge. He had taken a solemn vow to be obedient to his superiors, however. And so he accepted his next assignment: three years of teaching in Argentina. The first two would be in Santa Fe.

Jorge Bergoglio's friend Goma was also sent to Santa Fe. This city was across the Paraná River from the town of Paraná, where the Bergoglio family had first settled in Argentina. At the Colegio de la Inmaculada Concepción, a prestigious secondary school for boys, Jorge was assigned to teach psychology and literature. The rector of the school at that time was Father Ricardo O'Farrell.

Bergoglio's own secondary schooling had been focused on chemistry, so he had expected to teach science. However, he also had a good background in Spanish literature. From an early age he had read widely, including the classics, such as *El Cid* and *Don Quixote*. He had a special passion for Argentinian literature, going back to boyhood days when he'd first read the epic poem *El Gaucho Martín Fierro*.

Jorge Bergoglio was popular with his students, even though he demanded hard work from them. Tall and thin, with a face younger than his age of twenty-eight, Bergoglio was unusually serene and confident for a new teacher. His talks to his classes, given in a quiet voice, were entertaining as well as brilliant. He encouraged the boys to ask questions about the literature they were studying. As one student, Rogelio Pfirter, put it, "He made me discover infinite pleasures and possibilities in writing and reading . . . he stimulated me to think."

Bergoglio was fond of his students, and he understood that caring about each of them was the basis for good teaching. Many years later, he explained to interviewers how useless it was to "try to educate using only theoretical principles, without remembering that the most important thing is the person in front of you. . . . This does nothing for children."

When a student's behavior needed correction, Bergoglio chose a punishment that would actually motivate the boy to improve. For instance, one student, Roberto Poggio, was called in for slapping a younger student on the playing field. Instead of handing down a punishment himself, Bergoglio gathered a group of ten boys to question Roberto about the incident. The other boys were fair and nonjudgmental, and Roberto actually felt relieved after talking with them. He readily accepted their punishment: He had to apologize to the boy he had slapped, and he was suspended from sports for two weeks.

Another boy, Jorge Milia, performed outstandingly on his final exam in literature. But during the course, he had not bothered to hand in his classwork on time. Bergoglio recommended disciplining young Milia by reducing his final grade by a point. The purpose, he explained, was to remind the student that although he was bright and talented, it was still important for him to do his daily work patiently and painstakingly. Jorge Milia took the lesson to heart, and he later became a successful journalist.

Perhaps the most exciting moment during Bergoglio's two years of teaching in Santa Fe was the visit of the author Jorge Luis Borges to his classes. Bergoglio's idea was that the boys would benefit from direct contact with the writers of the literature they were studying. Bergoglio happened to have a secondhand connection to Borges: Borges's secretary, María Esther Vázquez, had taught him piano when he was ten years old. Still, it took some nerve to ask Borges, a world-renowned short-story writer, essayist, and poet, to travel from Buenos Aires to Santa Fe just to talk to a classroom of secondary school students.

But Bergoglio could be very persuasive. He must have communicated to the famous author his love for Argentine literature, including Borges's works, and his dedication to teaching. To prepare his students for the visit, he taught a whole unit on Borges.

After the visit in August 1965, which was a great success, Bergoglio had his students write their own short stories. He selected the eight best to send to Borges. The famous author graciously offered to write a prologue to the collection, *Original Stories*, which guaranteed it would be published. So the students, including Jorge Milia and Rogelio Pfirter, had the thrill of seeing their own writing in print in the same book with a piece of writing by Jorge Luis Borges.

The Colegio in Santa Fe was not only a renowned secondary school, but also a focus of popular piety, or religious devotion. In the school's chapel, built by the Jesuits in the seventeenth century, there was a painting of Mary, the mother of Jesus Christ, called *The Virgin of the Immaculate Conception*. From as long ago as 1636, the painting had been thought to work miracles. Water seeped from the picture, and believers dipped cotton in the water with which to anoint sick people. According to tradition, there had been miraculous cures.

Many Jesuits scoffed at such stories, but Jorge Bergoglio respected them. He knew what a deep impression it had made on him, as a child, to see and touch religious images and hear stories about the saints. He knew what an important aspect of faith the stories of miracles could be. For many people, especially the poor, they were a means of connecting with God.

Every morning before classes, Bergoglio would take

his students into the chapel, where the painting hung on the wall over the altar. He would lead them in bowing to Mary, to show deep reverence for her role in bringing God into the world in the person of her son Jesus.

CHAPTER 7

FATHER BERGOGLIO

THE TURMOIL FOLLOWING THE SECOND VATICAN Council was exciting to some young Jesuits in Argentina, including Jorge Bergoglio and his friends. But to others, it was confusing and discouraging. There were so many changes.

The Mass could now be said in Spanish instead of Latin. The priest officiating at the Mass could face the people in the church, instead of turning his back on them. Catholics were encouraged to read the Bible for themselves, instead of always letting a priest interpret it for them.

If so many traditions could be changed overnight, maybe other Church traditions were mistaken too. When so many rules were changing, why couldn't women become priests? Why did priests still have to be celibate?

Many young men questioned whether they were truly meant for the priesthood. Some left the order to get married. Others left to join the political conflict, which was growing more and more violent, in Argentina as well as in other Latin American countries. Of the novices who had begun training with Jorge Bergoglio in Córdoba in 1958, most dropped out of the program.

But Bergoglio was not typical of his classmates, and he held steady. In 1966, after two years of teaching in Santa Fe, he was transferred to Buenos Aires. There he taught for a year at another elite secondary school, the Colegio del Salvador. Again, he taught literature and psychology. The next year he returned to the Colegio Máximo in San Miguel to study theology for three years.

By this time, Bergoglio had been training to become a Jesuit priest for eight years. He was as determined as ever to complete the long course and become a full-fledged member of the Society of Jesus. For Jorge Bergoglio, the conclusions of Vatican II, especially as interpreted by Father Pedro

Arrupe, confirmed the teachings of Saint Ignatius Loyola.

Arrupe, superior general of the Society of Jesus, urged all Jesuits to renew their mission by going back to the original teachings of their founder. Jesuits should live in the world, but without giving in to worldly values of money, power, and prestige. Above all, Jesuits should support the poor, who deserved justice and peace.

During Jorge Bergoglio's last three years at the Colegio Máximo, his fellow students noticed that he was following a spare, simple way of life, not indulging in food or drink or other creature comforts. They also commented on how difficult it was to tell what he was thinking. They teased him that he was as inscrutable as the *Mona Lisa*, Leonardo da Vinci's famous portrait of a woman whose expression is hard to read.

Among the faculty at the Colegio Máximo were two Jesuits Bergoglio would find himself in serious disagreement with later. One was Franz Jalics, a philosophy teacher; another was Orlando Yorio, a theology teacher. Encouraged by Ricardo O'Farrell, the Jesuit provincial of Argentina at the time, Jalics and Yorio promoted the ideas and practice of liberation theology in their courses.

Liberation Theology

Liberation theology is an interpretation of the Christian religion that emphasizes the Church's responsibility for the poor and oppressed. The term became widely used after CELAM (the Conference of Latin American Bishops) at Medellín, Colombia, in 1968. This conference discussed how the recommendations of the Second Vatican Council should apply to Latin America. Although CELAM did not preach liberation theology as such, the conference summary stated a "preferential option for the poor."

This meant more than bringing the poor to church and giving them charity. It also meant that any social structures that kept these people poor were sinful. For instance, the poor deserved education. They needed to be set free not only from sin, but from illiteracy, and from ignorance of their legal rights.

And the leaders of the Church should not side with the wealthy and powerful. They should not live as the wealthy did, in luxury and privilege. As Pope Paul VI had said at the conclusion of the Second Vatican Council, Catholic bishops and clergy should be "poor, simple, humble, and lovable."

In Argentina and other Latin American countries, the Movement of Priests for the Third World put liberation theology into practice. They spread the Gospel (which means "good news") by leaving their rectories or residence houses and moving into impoverished communities. These "slum priests" taught the poor to read and to think for themselves

about what the Bible said. They taught that everyone deserved basic rights like sufficient food and
clean water.

Most followers of liberation theology believed
that they were simply returning to the ways of the
early Church, when the first Christians lived together,
worshipped together, and shared their goods.
But conservative politicians, as well as conservative church leaders, feared that liberation theology
would lead to the breakdown of society, even to violent revolution.

However, the teacher who was most important to Bergoglio
was still Father Miguel Fiorito, the dean of philosophy and
Bergoglio's spiritual director. Jorge Bergoglio was one of a
small group that formed around Fiorito, including Ernesto
López Rosas and Fernando Montes, Bergoglio's friend
from Chile. Fiorito, like Arrupe, taught that Jesuits needed
to return to the basics, as laid out by their founder, Saint
Ignatius Loyola. For one thing, they should go on individual retreats, rather than group retreats, to experience the
Exercises, a powerful means of opening oneself to God.

Also, Fiorito believed it was essential for Jesuits to
practice discernment of spirits. Fiorito was respected
throughout Argentina for his understanding of this
spiritual technique. He taught his students to set aside a

regular time to listen quietly for God's call, and to recognize temptations and distractions. Paying careful attention to their thoughts and feelings, they could realize which ones moved them closer to God and which ones pulled them away from God. It was especially important, Fiorito believed, to train novices in discernment.

During his own formation, Bergoglio had thought a great deal about how young men were trained as members of the Society of Jesus. He had ideas about how that process might be improved. Working with Father Fiorito, he became convinced that part of his calling was to become the novice master for the Jesuits of Argentina, the one who oversaw the training. In his last year at the Colegio Máximo, the Jesuit novice house was moved from Córdoba to San Miguel, close to the Colegio. Bergoglio was appointed assistant to the new novice master, Father Alfredo Estrella.

In December 1969, just before turning thirty-three, Jorge Mario Bergoglio was finally ordained as a priest. Before the ordination, he went on a retreat. He spent eight days in prayer and meditation, reviewing his life with gratitude for his many blessings, and with repentance for the times he had turned away from God's grace.

During one intense session, Bergoglio wrote down thoughts about his deepest beliefs. The final "I believe" began, "I believe in the surprise of each day."

On December 13, Bergoglio's family gathered in the chapel of the Colegio Máximo to witness his ordination. His mother was in the pews, as well as his grandmother Rosa and his brothers and sisters, but not Grandfather Giovanni, who had died in January 1964. Jorge and María Elena had grown even closer ever since their father's death, and he was a kind and protective big brother to her. Bergoglio's first-grade teacher, Estela Quiroga, also came to see her former "Jorgito" ordained.

Grandmother Rosa, who had taught Jorge the Catholic faith from the time he learned to walk, presented him with a special letter. She had written it some time ago, thinking that she might not live to see this day when he was first able to offer Holy Communion, to "hold in your consecrated hand Christ our Savior," as she put it.

The letter contained a blessing for "my grandchildren, to whom I gave the best of my heart," and spiritual advice for whatever hard times were to come. Jorge, now Father Bergoglio, put the precious letter in his breviary (a book of essential prayers, psalms, and other religious readings). He would keep Grandmother Rosa's letter close to him always.

Sadly, Mario Bergoglio, who would have been so happy and proud of his son on this day, had died years ago. But his mother, Regina, bitterly disappointed when Jorge chose the seminary over medical school, now seemed reconciled. At the ordination, she came forward and knelt for her son's blessing, and she kissed his hand.

Although Jorge Bergoglio was now a priest, he still had three more years of study at the Colegio, then study in Spain, and finally service in the Argentina province before he would be a full-fledged Jesuit. As he progressed through his long training, the political struggles in Argentina intensified. Many union members remembered fondly the prosperity and social reforms at the beginning of Juan Perón's presidency, and they planned and worked for Perón's return from exile in Spain. Meanwhile, the conservative governments still prevented the Peronist party from taking part in politics. One president of Argentina had quickly followed another, but whatever they promised, none of them could bring back economic good times.

Seizing power by a coup in 1966, General Juan Carlos Onganía had canceled elections entirely and disbanded the legislature. His government set out to restore Argentina's economy by controlling the trade unions and inviting foreign investment. Onganía froze workers' wages, lengthened their hours, and took away many of the rights they had gained, including the right to strike. Anyone who opposed these policies was in danger of arrest and imprisonment.

Onganía's policies did attract some foreign corporations, but the Argentinian economy suffered. Prices rose, and so did the number of unemployed. The workers' unions continued to organize protests and call for the return of Juan Perón. Perón, they believed, was on the side of the working classes.

The Catholic Church in Argentina split into factions, like the rest of the country. They took very different views of the recommendations of the Second Vatican Council and even the term "liberation theology." One faction, the Movement of Priests for the Third World, interpreted Vatican II's recommendations for reform as approval of a political ideology: socialism.

Father Carlos Mugica was a charismatic leader in this movement. He shared his life with the poor in one of the slums of Buenos Aires, called *villas miserias* ("misery villages"). The government had so little regard for this neighborhood that they gave it a number, Villa 31, rather than a name. The city of Buenos Aires did not provide clean water, electricity, or police protection to Villa 31; there were open sewers on the streets.

Father Mugica urged workers to stand up for their rights. He supported their efforts to form trade unions and bargain with owners. Mugica believed that Juan Perón would bring socialism to Argentina, and he worked for the former president's return.

An opposing faction of the Catholic Church in Argentina, including acting Archbishop Juan Carlos Aramburu, felt that the Church should act as a fortress against the attacks of modern culture. This faction was allied with Onganía's conservative government and the military. Aramburu forbade the priests in his archdiocese to express political opinions. However, Father Mugica and his followers ignored that order.

The majority of priests in Argentina, including Father Jorge Bergoglio, saw these political allegiances, left or right, as distractions from the Church's mission. The mandate of Vatican II, as Bergoglio understood it, was to refocus on spreading the Gospel. He was also inspired by the CELAM conference of the Latin American bishops in Medellín,

Colombia, in 1968. He believed that the Church in Latin America had a special understanding of Christianity to offer the world.

Conservatives criticized CELAM's declaration as based on Marxism, the theory behind communism. However, as Bergoglio would point out many years later, when he was archbishop of Buenos Aires, the CELAM positions did not come from the philosopher Karl Marx. They came from the earliest Christians, from Jesus's instructions to his followers in the Gospels. Those instructions were to share, rich and poor alike, and to spread the Good News of salvation.

In fact, the bishops at the CELAM conference were not sympathetic to communism, which they felt dehumanized people. And they did not agree with the Movement of Priests for the Third World, some of whom even called for a revolution to bring about a socialist government in Argentina. The CELAM bishops opposed violent revolution, even in a good cause.

In May 1969, the same year that Jorge Bergoglio was ordained a priest, thousands of university students and workers in Córdoba took to the streets in demonstrations. They were protesting the policies of General Onganía's government. Onganía sent troops to Córdoba, and they fired on and killed some of the protesters. But instead of putting down the unrest, the violence sparked even more protests around the country.

The Montoneros, a group intending to overthrow Onganía's government, judged (mistakenly) that ordinary Argentines were ready for armed rebellion. They took Onganía's attempts to repress the workers as a declaration of war. During the following years, they carried out many kidnappings and murders, and they exploded many bombs in public places. One of the people kidnapped and killed by Montoneros, in 1970, was General Pedro Aramburu, the former president who had driven Perón into exile in 1955.

As Father Jorge Bergoglio completed his last few months of theology studies at the Colegio Máximo, he watched the growing conflict with dismay. He loved his country passionately, but he did not take sides. He believed in the "preferential option for the poor"; he believed in peace and justice.

Like most of the priests in Argentina, Bergoglio did not believe that either violent rebellion or violent repression would bring about peace and justice. He was only thirty-three, but he had seen many governments of various political persuasions come and go. All of them had shown a "preferential option" for themselves, rather than for poor people. None of them had achieved lasting prosperity for the whole country.

In his spare time, Bergoglio listened to tango music and followed soccer. In fact, he never missed a soccer match when the San Lorenzo team was playing. He went to family barbecues and joked with his nephews and nieces. Among his other duties as a priest, he happily performed marriage ceremonies and baptisms for members of his extended family. And he trusted that whatever mission God had in mind for him would become clear.

CHAPTER 8

THE SCHOOL OF THE HEART

UP UNTIL AGE THIRTY-FOUR, JORGE BERGOGLIO had hardly traveled outside Argentina. He had left the country only once, for his juniorate year in Chile. But in 1970, for the next and last stage in his Jesuit training, he journeyed across the Atlantic Ocean and into the Northern Hemisphere, to Spain.

This was a chance for Bergoglio to actually visit the many places he had only read about. The center for the Jesuit tertianship, as this last stage was called, was in Alcalá de Henares, a city near Madrid. Bergoglio and twelve other students, some from Spain and some from as far away as Japan, lived here for five months.

Saint Ignatius of Loyola himself, the founder of the Society of Jesus, had once lived and taught in Alcalá. It was also the birthplace of Miguel de Cervantes, author of the classic Spanish novel *Don Quixote*. Furthermore, the history of the area went all the way back to the first centuries of Christianity. The medieval cathedral at Alcalá was dedicated to two Christian boys, Saint Justus and Saint Pastor, who had been killed by order of the Roman emperor Diocletian in the fourth century.

But the main purpose of this last stage of formation was to bring the Jesuits-in-training back to what Saint Ignatius called "the school of the heart." Bergoglio had spent twelve years developing his mind through studying and teaching. Now he sought, on a deeper level, to confirm his call to the Jesuit mission.

As when they were novices, Bergoglio and the other students at Alcalá concentrated on the basics of the Jesuit way. Again, they spent one month in a retreat devoted to the Spiritual Exercises, the series of meditations and prayers developed by Saint Ignatius. However, this time they followed the Spiritual Exercises in individual retreats, rather than as a group. Bergoglio felt that he was undergoing the Exercises as Ignatius Loyola had intended.

In Alcalá, the tertian students also steeped themselves in the original writings of Saint Ignatius. And as when they were novices, they performed humble tasks of service. They visited the inmates of a nearby prison and waited on the patients at a hospital. At that same hospital, Ignatius himself had once cared for the sick and worked as a cook.

This was an intense program, but the men also had time off to travel around Spain. Bergoglio usually made these side trips with a Spanish student, Jesús María Alemany. Alemany was impressed with Bergoglio's quietness and simplicity, as well as his intelligence. The Argentinian had a way of keeping himself in the background without being standoffish. At the same time, he was good company, friendly and amusing to talk with. And he was crazy about soccer.

The tertian stage was not only a time for Jorge Bergoglio to decide whether or not to make his final commitment to the Society of Jesus. It was also a time for the Society to judge whether or not Bergoglio was truly suited for the Jesuit life. During the years of his formation, many Jesuits in Argentina, as well as the superior general in Rome, Father Arrupe, had noticed Jorge Bergoglio's outstanding qualities. Besides his intelligence, he was a natural leader with a deep spiritual life.

Bergoglio seemed like just the man who was needed to breathe new life into the program of Jesuit formation. Around the world, the Society of Jesus had been shaken, like the rest of the Church, by young men dropping out of training and older men leaving the priesthood. In Argentina, the loss of Jesuits was even worse than in other countries.

In 1971, at the end of his tertianship, Bergoglio returned to Argentina from Spain. His Jesuit training was complete, although he would not take his final vows for two more years. In April, Father Ricardo O'Farrell, the provincial or head of the Jesuits of Argentina, appointed him novice master for the province. This was a position of great responsibility, especially for a Jesuit who had not yet taken his final vows. Bergoglio was thirty-five, a young age to be entrusted with bringing along the next generation of Jesuits.

However, Bergoglio did have experience as assistant novice master. And he was respected and trusted by an authority on Jesuit spirituality, Father Miguel Fiorito at the Colegio Máximo. Father O'Farrell, the provincial, also knew Bergoglio well, because he had been the rector of the secondary school during Jorge Bergoglio's two years of teaching in Santa Fe. He had seen that Bergoglio had a gift for leading and nurturing young minds.

The Jesuit novice center had been moved from Córdoba to San Miguel, close to the Colegio Máximo. Bergoglio lived there in the novice house, the Villa Barilari, and applied his understanding of the Second Vatican Council's call for reform. For some Catholics, reforming the Church meant throwing out traditions and making the Church conform to modern culture. But to Bergoglio, reform meant recognizing and responding to modern culture, but not allowing it to control the Church's behavior.

Under his leadership, the novices led a simple and humble life. They wore black cassocks, long close-fitting garments. Along with their disciplined routine of prayer and worship, they did hard physical work, such as gardening and pig tending.

Novice Master Bergoglio led the way, wading into the muck of pigpens in his rubber boots. The pigpen, he told a visitor, was a good place to pray. God had created the entire world, not only the clean and lofty parts. So God was to be found in the lowliest places.

Bergoglio sent his novices out to the shantytowns around San Miguel, to spend time with the poor. The students joked that he would check their shoes for dust (a sign that they had really walked the dirt streets in the slums) when they returned. Bergoglio wanted them not only to teach the poor the basics of the Catholic faith, but also to get to know the people. This meant chatting, meeting their families, sharing a gourd of maté.

Bergoglio also wanted his novices to practice popular piety, or religious devotion, such as kissing the statues in the chapel and making pilgrimages to holy sites. Since poor people understood their Catholic faith through these practices, he believed, a priest-in-training needed to experience popular piety for himself. Besides, Bergoglio felt more and more sure that in some ways, poor people had a better grip on the faith than distinguished theologians did.

Throughout the program, Bergoglio sought to introduce his Jesuits-in-training to the deep spirituality of their founder, Ignatius of Loyola. It was less about following strict rules and more about opening themselves to God's will. Rather than controlling the novices' hearts and minds himself, Bergoglio wanted to help them give themselves up to God.

Bergoglio sympathized with the novices' inner struggles, remembering his doubts during his seminary days. And his own brother Alberto had begun to follow in Jorge's steps to become a Jesuit but had dropped out. If a novice was considering leaving the program, Bergoglio encouraged him to discern the right choice without feeling guilty.

While Bergoglio was directing the Jesuit novice program in San Miguel, a friend of his was living out a version of liberation theology nearby. Sergio Gobulin, a student at the Colegio Máximo, decided to move into one of the slums of San Miguel. He was not a priest or even a churchgoer, but he believed in peace and justice. He worked to educate the poor, to bring clean water into the slum, and to pave the dirt roads. Bergoglio was impressed with Gobulin's project, and he came and stayed several days with him to learn more about it.

Still following a simple way of life, Bergoglio allowed himself a *few* indulgences. One of them was music: classical music and the tango. He knew the tango singers of this time as well as those of his teenage years. He was an admirer of the songs of Azucena Maizani, the first popular woman tango artist. When she died in 1970, he gave her the last rites.

Along with his responsibilities as Jesuit novice master, Father Bergoglio acted as chaplain to the Iron Guard, a moderate-right Peronist student group at the University of el Salvador in Buenos Aires. They took their name from Puerta de Hierro, or Iron Gate, the neighborhood in Madrid where Juan Perón lived in exile. They believed that they, not the rebel Montoneros or the extreme rightists who backed Onganía's dictatorship, were the ones who understood Peronism correctly.

During his two years as novice master, Bergoglio was appointed vice rector of the Colegio Máximo. He also became a professor of pastoral theology, teaching such subjects as how to give homilies (brief sermons), how to conduct Mass, and how to care for the needs of the people in a parish. And he was appointed a consultor, or adviser, to Provincial Ricardo O'Farrell.

By this time, the more conservative, mostly older Jesuits in Argentina were on the point of rebellion against the leadership of Ricardo O'Farrell. They complained that Jesuits were supposed to be "contemplatives in action," but O'Farrell had skimped on the contemplative side. Since his appointment as provincial in 1969, Father O'Farrell had been sympathetic to the Movement of Priests for the Third World. He encouraged Jesuits, including Orlando Yorio and Franz Jalics, who wanted to follow Father Carlos Mugica's example of living and working with the poor. Rather than live in Jesuit residences, these priests wanted to form "base communities" in the slums, the *villas miserias*.

O'Farrell also allowed changes in what was taught, and who was allowed to teach, at the Colegio Máximo. Under the direction of Yorio, the vice dean of theology, courses in the humanities were dropped in favor of courses in political theory and sociology. Bergoglio, who considered the humanities so important, was one of those disturbed by these changes. Also, some of these new courses were taught by priests who acted as chaplains to the Montoneros, the rebels fighting to overturn the military dictatorship.

The conservative Jesuits thought Father O'Farrell's policies were actually endangering the whole Society of Jesus of Argentina. They accused him of linking the Jesuits to liberation theology and the political movement for social change. They were afraid that all priests who worked with the poor, or even all Jesuits, would be viewed as dangerous revolutionaries. In 1972 the conservative Jesuits petitioned Father Arrupe, their superior general in Rome, to remove Father O'Farrell from the position of provincial.

O'Farrell was just four years into his six-year term, but it was true that during those years, the order had fallen into disarray. Young men were no longer joining the Jesuits— the number of novices had dropped to three. Furthermore, many full-fledged Jesuits had left the priesthood to marry or to join the Montoneros: And the remaining Jesuits in Argentina were not in harmony, but divided into angry factions. Considering all this, Father Arrupe agreed to choose a new provincial for Argentina.

Two years earlier, in 1970, President Onganía's government had lost control of the country. A series of acting presidents were appointed by the military. Finally, in 1973, elections were held and the Peronists won. But the Peronist party itself was deeply split between left and right.

On June 20, Perón and his third wife, María Estela (known as Isabel), were due to arrive at Ezeiza airport, outside Buenos Aires. Two million people gathered to await their hero's return, expecting to celebrate. Instead, a troop of far-right gunmen concealed on the speaking platform fired on left-wing groups, including the Montoneros, killing thirteen or more and wounding hundreds. The huge crowd scattered, and Perón's plane had to divert to another airport.

This incident was a bad sign for Argentinians' hopes that Juan Perón could pull the country together. Nevertheless, in September 1973, eighteen years after he had been forced from office, Perón stepped into the presidency of Argentina again.

In April 1973 Jorge Bergoglio took his final vows to become a full-fledged member of the Society of Jesus. He promised special allegiance to the pope. He also promised never to seek to rise in the hierarchy of the Church. For a gifted, dedicated priest like Bergoglio, ambition was a particular spiritual danger. It would be all too easy for him to be promoted higher and higher in the ranks of the Church, to become full of his own importance and wisdom, and to mistake his own will for the will of God.

Only a few months after Bergoglio had made his final vows, Father Arrupe appointed him to replace Ricardo

O'Farrell as provincial of the Argentine Jesuits. It was very unusual for a Jesuit as young as Bergoglio to be given the heavy responsibility of provincial. He would be in charge of every Jesuit and every Jesuit institution in the entire country. Normally, O'Farrell would have been replaced by Father Luis Escribano, an older, more experienced Jesuit. But Escribano had recently died in a car accident.

In Bergoglio's favor, he had already served as novice master, professor, and provincial consultor. Also, many in the Society of Jesus, including the highly respected Father Fiorito, believed he had the spiritual maturity and leadership qualities for the job. And perhaps, the thinking went, a younger man was needed to connect with the younger generation.

Jorge Bergoglio accepted his new assignment. On July 31, 1973, he became provincial for the Society of Jesus in Argentina.

At the same time as the turmoil among the Jesuits, political upheavals shook governments all over Latin America. On the western side of the Andes, in Chile, the socialist Salvador Allende had been elected president in 1970. But in 1973 a coup led by General Augusto Pinochet overthrew Allende's government. The military junta immediately executed hundreds of socialists, to the shock of the international community. In Uruguay, too, a military dictatorship seized power in 1973. In Nicaragua, the Sandinista rebels fought against Anastasio Somoza's repressive rule.

Peronism, Left and Right

"Peronism" is usually taken to mean a political movement favoring socialism—equal distribution of wealth and national ownership of industries. But actually, former president Perón favored whatever political ideology might bring him back to power in Argentina. During his exile in the 1960s, he allowed very different groups, with very different ideas of government, to call themselves Peronist.

One branch of the outlawed Peronist party, the Montonero Peronist Movement, was openly leftist. They carried on an increasingly violent guerilla struggle against the military dictatorship of Argentina. The Montoneros' goal was to transform Argentina into a socialist country like Cuba, and they thought that Perón shared their goal. Perón encouraged that impression by making favorable comments about Fidel Castro of Cuba and by meeting with Ernesto "Che" Guevara, a hero for the Montoneros.

Another political faction in Argentina, also claiming to be Peronist, was right-wing. They agreed with Onganía's capitalistic economic policies. Their goal was to save Argentina, capitalism, and the Catholic Church from atheistic communism.

In April 1973, when elections were allowed in Argentina again, Hector Campora of the Peronist party won the presidency. It seemed that socialism had won as well. Campora released Montoneros who had been imprisoned by Onganía, and he appointed many Montoneros to government positions.

Juan Perón himself returned that June and easily won a special election. But as president, Perón adjusted his political views to match the realities of 1973. He did not side with the workers and their labor unions, as he had in the 1940s. Instead, Perón sided with the political right wing—the conservative bishops in the Church, the wealthy upper classes, and the military.

The socialist Peronists began telling a bitter joke: Perón's luxury automobile comes to a fork in the road. The driver asks, "Which way, General?" Perón answers, "The usual. Signal left and turn right."

Seeing the Montoneros and other left-wing revolutionaries as the largest threat to his power, Perón allowed a right-wing paramilitary group, the Alianza Anticomunista Argentina, to take action. In 1973 the Triple A, as this group was called, began patrolling the streets with death squads.

Most Argentinian voters hoped that Perón, whatever his politics, would at last bring peace and economic recovery to the country. But in July 1974, less than a year after his election, Juan Perón died of a heart attack. His wife, Isabel, was the vice president, but she had no experience in government, and no natural talent for leading. In spite of this, Isabel Perón became the next president.

CHAPTER 9
GOD'S HOLY FAITHFUL PEOPLE

MANY YEARS LATER, JORGE BERGOGLIO COM-
mented to an interviewer on his appointment as the
young leader of the Society of Jesus of Argentina. "I was
only thirty-six," he said. "That was crazy." But at the time,
Bergoglio felt fairly confident, because he saw a clear
goal. *His* mission was to refocus the Jesuits under his care
on *their* mission. In his first message to the province, in
February 1974, Bergoglio urged Jesuits to pay attention
to what was truly important to the poor people of the
Catholic Church, "God's holy faithful people."

"This people believes in the resurrection and the life: salvation, work, bread, everyday understanding in their families," said Bergoglio. "For their country, what they believe in is peace." By "peace," he explained, he did not mean that poor people should be resigned to being exploited and oppressed. The peace he had in mind would be "the fruit of justice."

Bergoglio had a problem with ideological theories, both left-wing and right-wing, about what was good for people. The trouble with these theories, Bergoglio thought, was that they ignored the actual people. As one of Bergoglio's students, Hugo Salaberry, expressed it, Bergoglio "always is concerned about the concrete person, victim of injustices of poverty. He always knew people by name and because of this people love him a lot."

The other focus that the Society of Jesus badly needed, Bergoglio believed, was returning to the original teachings of Saint Ignatius Loyola. These would be his guiding principles for the years ahead.

In August 1973, shortly after Jorge Bergoglio became provincial, Superior General Arrupe arrived from Rome. The two men traveled around the country together, and

Bergoglio came to admire the older Jesuit even more. He noted how much he prayed, and where he prayed—sitting on the ground, as Arrupe had learned in Japan during his missionary years.

As they traveled, the superior general and the young provincial discussed the serious problems facing Bergoglio now. A major problem was how the Jesuits of Argentina could remain true to their mission and survive, in the midst of ever-increasing violence.

If Bergoglio and Arrupe hadn't already known how bad things were, they would have been convinced by their visit to La Rioja. The Jesuits had a close connection with La Rioja, a city and province in the northwest of Argentina. Their missionaries ran several parishes of impoverished people in remote areas of the province. Pope Paul VI had asked Arrupe to visit Enrique Angelelli, the bishop of La Rioja, to show support.

Bishop Angelelli had taken part in the Second Vatican Council in the 1960s, and he put its recommendations into practice in his diocese. He believed deeply that the Church must work with the poor to combat social injustice. With Angelelli's approval, his priests had helped landless farmworkers organize into unions and take over water reservoirs on private land. Recently Angelelli had been stoned by a mob representing the wealthy landowners.

When Arrupe and Bergoglio flew into La Rioja airport, they found that it was not safe to get out of their plane. Another mob, sent by the landowners, was waiting for them, so they had to sit on the runway. Eventually Arrupe and Bergoglio managed to sneak out of their plane and into Bishop Angelelli's car, avoiding a confrontation.

The Jesuits of Argentina faced another serious problem, which Arrupe discussed with Bergoglio: they were losing money as well as manpower. They could not afford to keep up all their institutions and the buildings that housed them. With Arrupe's approval, Bergoglio decided to sell several valuable properties, including the former novice house in Córdoba.

One major financial burden for the province was the Jesuits' University of el Salvador in Buenos Aires. The university was deeply in debt. Also, like the Colegio Máximo, it had become dominated by leftist teaching. The courses, the professors, and the students were Marxist. Courses in the humanities had been dropped.

Again with Father Arrupe's approval, Bergoglio decided to hand over the University of el Salvador to people he knew and trusted, former members of the Peronist Iron Guard. Liberation theology courses were discontinued, and humanities courses, including Argentine history and literature, were restored. Bergoglio hoped these changes would remove the emphasis on ideology and politics, especially the trend toward violence, and focus on the "people's theology." But Jesuits like Orlando Yorio, deeply committed to the Marxist version of liberation theology, felt that he was betraying them.

Above all, Arrupe and Bergoglio agreed on his overarching goal: to unify the Jesuits of Argentina. This was important in itself, but it was also necessary to the goal of attracting new men to the Society of Jesus. And in order for the Jesuits in Argentina to continue their teaching and missionary work, there must always be new Jesuits in training.

Bergoglio had long had a special concern for the training program. Although he was no longer novice master, he kept in close touch with the program. He moved his office from Buenos Aires to the Colegio Máximo, near the novice house, and he visited them once a week.

The new novice master, Father Andrés Swinnen, continued Bergoglio's policy of setting the novices to work spreading the Gospel. They were sent into the working-class suburbs of San Miguel to gather children and teach them the basics of the Catholic faith. They were also instructed to notice what the poor people in the neighborhoods needed, and to return with food, medicines, and blankets. When a novice reported severe hunger among the children in one poor section, Bergoglio immediately set up a soup kitchen serving two hundred. Children of the slums, most of whom had never seen the nearby seashore, needed a chance to play in the fresh air, and they were taken on outings to the beach.

As when Bergoglio was novice master, the novices were asked to practice the same customs of popular piety that Bergoglio had learned from his grandmother Rosa. But Jesuits traditionally prided themselves on their intellectual accomplishments, and many of them thought it was superstitious to venerate saints, say novenas, and make pilgrimages to shrines. They did not believe the story of the miracle of Our Lady of Luján, who was said to have stopped the oxcart from carrying her away from Buenos Aires.

These Jesuits were outraged by Bergoglio's emphasis on popular piety. However, under Bergoglio's policies, the number of novices increased year after year. And so did the number of Jesuits who completed their training.

As a young man, Bergoglio had hoped to be sent to Japan as a Jesuit missionary. But now he understood that missionaries were badly needed in his own country. In spite of the fact that the Spanish had brought Christianity to Latin America in the sixteenth century, there were many people, especially in northern Argentina, who knew little about the Catholic faith.

During the Jesuit trainees' juniorate year, Bergoglio had them sent out on missions to remote areas of Argentina. They went from village to village, sharing the poverty of the people and their piety, the way they experienced the Christian faith. Bergoglio increased the missions in La Rioja, Bishop Angelelli's diocese, and he sent Jesuits as far north as the border with Bolivia.

Another decision for which Bergoglio was bitterly criticized was closing the base communities that O'Farrell had encouraged, bringing the "slum priests" back into Jesuit residences. Bergoglio certainly wanted the priests under his direction to spend time with the poor people. But he also felt it was important for Jesuits to live with one another.

This, he believed, would help bring the province together and keep them mindful of the wider Jesuit mission.

Bergoglio also was very concerned for the safety of the priests in the base communities. After Juan Perón's death in July 1974, Buenos Aires collapsed into a rhythm of rebel terrorism followed by government counterterrorism, with the rest of the population trying to stay safe. Left-wing militants and right-wing militants slaughtered one another, as well as the civilians who sympathized with one side or the other, and even innocent bystanders.

Father Carlos Mugica, a leader in the Movement of Priests for the Third World, was one of the first "slum priests" to become a martyr. Mugica did not advocate violence, but he did officiate at the funerals of Montoneros, against the orders of his conservative bishop. For several years Bishop Juan Carlos Aramburu had advised Mugica to leave the priesthood, and by 1974, he was threatening to defrock him. On May 11, 1974, Mugica was shot dead outside Cristo Obrero (Christ the Worker), a church in Villa 31, by right-wing paramilitaries.

Faced with such a threat to the priests in his care, Bergoglio began to close the base communities. By the end of 1974, the only one remaining was the community of his former professors, Orlando Yorio and Franz Jalics, in the Bajo Flores section of Buenos Aires. It was very dangerous for them to stay there, and many people besides Bergoglio warned them to leave.

But Yorio and Jalics resisted taking orders from Bergoglio, a younger man and a former student of theirs. Besides, they believed deeply in their community in the slums. During 1975, they tried instead to make some arrangement to start a new branch of the Society of Jesus, in which they would not be under Bergoglio's direction.

During these tense years, Bergoglio found comfort in the time he spent with his grandmother Rosa. By now she was elderly and frail, cared for by nuns in San Miguel. Bergoglio was usually nearby, at the Colegio Máximo or at the novice center, and he visited her often. During her last hours, he held her in his arms until she died.

Meanwhile, Isabel Perón's presidency plunged toward disaster. The real power in her government seemed to be José López Rega, her minister of social welfare. López Rega was the founder of the deadly Triple A, and he supported them with money from the social welfare department. Before the end of 1974, the Triple A paramilitaries had murdered three hundred people, including Father Mugica. The next year, they accomplished four hundred fifty assassinations and two thousand kidnappings.

On the other side of what was now civil war, the People's Revolutionary Army (ERP) launched a series of attacks against military bases in Tucuman, in the northwest of Argentina. The Montoneros, having been shut out of Perón's government, returned to guerrilla action with assassinations, bombings, and kidnappings. Both leftist groups raised millions of dollars of ransom money, which was used to buy heavy weaponry.

With rebellion raging, Isabel Perón issued a decree legalizing kidnapping, torture, and execution without trial. The Montoneros spray-painted their scornful comment about President Isabel Perón on walls throughout the country: "If Evita [Perón] were alive, she would be a Montonero."

Frightened by the widespread violence, foreign investors pulled their money out of Argentina. Inflation ballooned, making workers' wages worth almost nothing. In any case, great numbers of them were unemployed.

As for the general population of Argentina, they longed

for somebody to restore law and order. Civil leaders urged the military to step in and take over the government. All the political parties, except the communists, believed that a coup was necessary.

Knowing that the military takeover could happen any day, Jorge Bergoglio was concerned for a friend of his, an attorney named Alicia Oliveira. She had become Argentina's first woman criminal judge. She was also one of the few lawyers brave enough to defend citizens whose human rights had been violated, such as by imprisonment without trial. As a result, the government's security forces were targeting her as a dangerous subversive.

In a way, theirs was an odd friendship. Bergoglio was a deeply committed Jesuit priest, while Oliveira, a single mother of three, had a low opinion of the Catholic Church. However, they were both intelligent people with a sharp sense of humor, and they had an affectionate respect for each other. She had asked Bergoglio to be the godfather of her youngest son.

Oliveira was impressed with the action Bergoglio took at the secondary school in Buenos Aires where her sons studied. The Jesuit-run Colegio del Salvador, where Bergoglio had taught in 1966, had traditionally been separated into two schools in the same building, with one entrance for the students from wealthy families and another for the scholarship students. "When Bergoglio was provincial," she said later, "he closed down the free school and moved all the poor children into the rich one. He did not tell the parents."

Worried for Oliveira's safety, Bergoglio invited her to move into the Colegio del Salvador herself. She thanked him but refused, adding jokingly, "I'd rather go to prison than live with priests."

As it turned out, that was a grimmer joke than she could guess. And no one, including Jorge Bergoglio, imagined the horrors to come.

CHAPTER 10

THE DIRTY WAR

ON MARCH 24, 1976, TANKS ROLLED INTO THE streets of Buenos Aires. Military helicopters chopped the air over the Plaza de Mayo, and troops occupied every major city in Argentina. A military junta led by Jorge Rafael Videla, Emilio Eduardo Massera, and Orlando Ramón Agosti marched into the Casa Rosada, the national offices, and seized control of the government.

That same day, the junta's security forces arrested hundreds of workers, union leaders, university students, and other suspected leftists. Videla, acting as president, announced a new government with a harmless-sounding name, the National Reorganization Process. His promise to "eradicate subversion" was a truer indication of their intentions. But only Videla's inner circle knew that in order to wipe out the rebellion—about two thousand remaining left-wing guerrillas—he expected to kill five thousand Argentinians. And not even Videla predicted that in the end, *El Proceso*, as the National Reorganization Process was known, would kill many thousands more.

The dictatorship carried out their worst human rights abuses in secrecy, so it was a long time before most Argentinians understood what was happening. "At the beginning," Bergoglio told a journalist later, "little or nothing was known; we became aware gradually." He knew that many people were being arrested, but he did not understand right away how savagely ruthless the Videla government was.

But Bergoglio was not surprised when, shortly after the coup, the government fired Alicia Oliveira from her position as a judge. He sent her flowers, with a note of appreciation for her judicial work. He didn't sign the card, but she recognized his handwriting, and she was touched.

Realizing her danger, Oliveira finally went into hiding at a friend's apartment. Bergoglio picked her up twice a week and took her to the Colegio del Salvador so that she could see her children.

A few months after the coup, the government's security forces murdered three priests and two seminarians in the Church of San Patricio in Buenos Aires. They were shot in front of the altar and left with a note that the killing was revenge for the recent bombing of a police station by the Montoneros. Bergoglio knew two of the murdered men personally—he was spiritual director to Alfredo Kelly, one of the priests, and Emilio Barletti, one of the seminarians, was a student at the Colegio Máximo.

In that same month, July 1976, Bishop Angelelli and the head of the air force base in Rioja came into conflict. To punish Angelelli, the air force head had two of the bishop's priests kidnapped and murdered. Their bodies were left on a railroad track with a warning: a list of the troublesome priests who would be killed next.

Angelelli publicly denounced the kidnapping and murders. A few weeks later, in August, the police reported that Angelelli had died in a car crash. In fact, by orders from the military, the bishop's truck had been driven off the road. He had been beaten to death.

Bergoglio was in Central America at the time, attending a meeting of Jesuit provincials. But when he heard of Angelelli's assassination, he returned to Argentina. He was already sheltering at the Colegio Máximo three of Angelelli's seminary students who had been working in the slums. It was becoming clear to him that the military dictatorship intended to go far beyond fighting the Montoneros and other rebels. As far as the junta was concerned, anyone even working with the poor was dangerous and should be exterminated.

One of Angelelli's young men, Miguel La Civita, told later how Bergoglio had comforted him and the other seminarians in their grief and terror over Angelelli's murder. Bergoglio also instructed La Civita and the other two on how to help with the many people he was hiding at the Colegio Máximo. They had to be careful, because some of the Jesuits living at the Colegio were army chaplains and not trustworthy.

Bergoglio's refugees were supposedly on "silent retreat," in a part of the college shut off from the rest. La Civita sometimes took meals to the retreat rooms, but he knew not to ask questions. He gathered, however, that the "retreatants" were waiting until they could be smuggled out of Argentina with fake papers.

In fact, Bergoglio was part of a whole international system for rescuing people targeted by the junta. They took them to hiding places, such as the retreat wing of the Colegio Máximo. They arranged for false travel documents. And they sent them on to Brazil or another neighboring country.

The refugees were still not out of danger as long as they remained in South America, because Brazil, as well as Chile, Uruguay, and Paraguay, were also ruled by military dictatorships. These governments cooperated, through a program called Operation Condor, to stamp out "subversives." But the Jesuits managed to shelter the fugitives until it was safe for them to board a plane for Europe.

Jorge Bergoglio helped personally in many of these escapes—a very dangerous thing to do. He drove several of the refugees to the airport. In the case of one man who looked somewhat like him, he bought the man a priest's suit and collar, gave him his own identity papers, and drove him to the border.

Bergoglio had no use for any political ideology, left or right, that was willing for innocent people to suffer. He heard the leaders of the junta calling the leftists a "cancer" that must be cut from the national body by surgery. He heard the leftist Montoneros justifying their bombings, kidnappings, and killings as "clean," in contrast to the dictatorship's violence. For Bergoglio, and for God as Bergoglio understood God, the individual person came before ideology.

However, Bergoglio worked to keep in touch with all political sides, and he was very skillful at not letting anyone know what he was thinking. As Jesuit provincial, he had many sources of information, because the Jesuits themselves covered the whole political spectrum. On the one hand, there were priests, like Yorio, who encouraged the Montoneros; on the other hand, there were priests who approved of and supported the dictatorship.

Quietly using all his resources, Bergoglio was able to save many innocent people. One of these was a former theology student at the Colegio Máximo, Sergio Gobulin. Sergio and his wife, Ana, were friends of Bergoglio's; in fact, he had performed their marriage ceremony.

In October 1976, the couple was teaching in a slum. Taking this work with the poor as a sign of leftist sympathies, the security forces kidnapped Sergio. They took him to a secret prison, where he was badly beaten. Bergoglio arranged for Ana to go into hiding, and he worked for weeks, meeting with influential officers, to get Sergio released.

Rescuing people marked by the junta was not only dangerous; it could be sickening. Miguel La Civita, one of the seminarians under Bergoglio's protection, happened to be present when a high-ranking officer from the air force came to meet with Bergoglio. Bergoglio, showing no sign of disgust or horror, had refreshments served. He calmly told the officer that Sergio Gobulin had done nothing wrong, and he must be released.

At the end of the interview, Bergoglio asked La Civita to show the visitor out. When the seminarian returned to the office, he found Bergoglio vomiting. "Sometimes when you're done talking to these people," he explained to La Civita, "you've got to throw up."

A few days later, Sergio was released—badly beaten, but alive. While he was recovering in the hospital, Bergoglio warned the couple to flee the country as soon as possible. Bergoglio was able to help with their escape, through his connections with the Italian vice-consul in Buenos Aires.

Another good friend of Bergoglio's in danger from the junta was his old boss and mentor at the laboratory, Esther Ballestrino de Careaga. Esther helped found a protest group, the Mothers of the Plaza de Mayo, women whose children had been kidnapped by the junta. These women held their first rally in April 1977 in the Plaza de Mayo, the main square of Buenos Aires.

Then Esther's own daughter Ana María was kidnapped by the military. Esther somehow managed to get Ana María released and smuggled her out of the country to refuge in Sweden. But Esther herself returned to Buenos Aires and continued leading the Mothers of the Plaza de Mayo. Their weekly demonstrations in front of the Casa Rosada, the presidential office building, drew international attention and began to embarrass the government.

In December 1977, Esther and eleven others were kidnapped at their meeting place, the Church of Santa Cruz. Bergoglio, horrified, worked frantically to find out where Esther had been taken and to have her released. But this time, in spite of all his sources, he couldn't get any information. Meanwhile, the military drugged Esther and the other prisoners, loaded them into a plane, and dropped them into the ocean to drown. No one knew what had happened until much later, when their bodies washed up on the shore.

So this was what General Videla meant by "national

reorganization." The junta was not aiming merely to restore order in Argentina. They intended to wipe out every trace of resistance to their rule. Anyone who showed the slightest left-leaning sympathy could be arrested, tortured, and killed without trial or any official explanation—they would simply be *desaparecido*, "disappeared." The government was controlling the country by terror.

Jorge Bergoglio did all he could to help those who were persecuted by the dictatorship. Alicia Oliveira urged him to speak out publicly against the government's abuse of power, but Bergoglio did not think that was the way he could do the most good. If he spoke out, he would most likely be assassinated, as Bishop Angelelli had been.

Bergoglio, with his deep confidence in the Christian faith, was not afraid to die. But he believed he would be more helpful to innocent victims if he kept his opinions to himself and worked undercover. Besides, as leader of the Society of Jesus in Argentina, he felt a special responsibility to protect the Jesuits.

And *their* special responsibility, in his view, was to obey him, their leader. In becoming a Jesuit, each one of them had vowed obedience: to the pope, to their superior general in Rome, and to the leader of the Jesuit province of Argentina. Bergoglio had taken on the heavy burden of deciding what was best for his men, but they had to obey.

Bergoglio feared for the priests doing work in poor neighborhoods. He warned them not to travel back from the slums alone after dark, when they would be easy targets for the death squads. One of the priests he warned was Juan Carlos Scannone. Besides working with the poor, he was a professor of theology at the Colegio Máximo, and he was wrongly labeled Marxist by the government. But Scannone took Bergoglio's advice and survived.

During 1976, even before the takeover of the military dictatorship, Bergoglio was especially worried about Father Orlando Yorio and Father Franz Jalics. All the other base communities had been closed and the other Jesuit priests moved into clergy residences. But Yorio and Jalics stubbornly remained living in Villa 11.14, one of the *villas miserias* of Buenos Aires.

Bergoglio knew the government was convinced that all "slum priests" were Montoneros and that, worse, they were turning the slum dwellers into Montoneros. As Bergoglio saw it, these priests were a danger to themselves and to the poor people they lived with. They could also endanger other Jesuits, by giving the impression that the whole Society of Jesus supported the Montoneros. Sooner or later, they would be kidnapped and imprisoned, or shot on the street as Father Carlos Mugica had been.

Bergoglio had many discussions with Yorio and Jalics. One possible compromise was for the two priests to move to a Jesuit residence, but continue to work in Villa 11.14, in Bajo Flores. But Yorio and Jalics were determined to remain in their base community.

In February 1976 Bergoglio traveled to Rome and discussed the problem with Father Arrupe, the superior general. He returned with a letter from Arrupe, ordering the community to be dissolved, and sending Yorio and Jalics to assignments outside Argentina. Angry, the two priests decided to resign from the Jesuits and found their own religious order.

By this time, it was the middle of March. The military seized power a few days later. Some of the priests and lay workers in Villa 11.14 listened to the many warnings, and they left the community. Of the lay teachers who stayed, four were kidnapped by the military and disappeared. But Yorio and Jalics stayed on until May 23. On that day a troop of marines stormed into their house and arrested them, along with six more lay teachers.

This was exactly what Bergoglio had been afraid of. He found out quickly that Yorio and Jalics were being held at the detention center at the Navy Mechanics School (ESMA), and he used all his contacts to try to have them freed. He even managed to speak with two of the junta leaders, Videla and Massera.

The military did decide they had made a mistake in arresting these two priests. But now they hesitated to let them go, for fear of what they could reveal. So Yorio and Jalics spent five grim months, blindfolded and handcuffed, in a secret location.

Meanwhile, some powerful people in high places—perhaps Pope Paul VI, perhaps U.S. presidential candidate Jimmy Carter—quietly put pressure on the government of Argentina. Finally, in October, the two priests were drugged, flown by helicopter to a deserted area outside Buenos Aires, and left on the ground. When they regained consciousness, they made their way to a phone and called Bergoglio.

Bergoglio knew his phone was tapped by the security forces, so he immediately instructed Yorio and Jalics not to tell him where they were. The junta might still have them shot on the street, to keep them from talking. Rather, they should send someone in person to give him that information, and he would have them picked up and taken to a safe place.

Afterward, Bergoglio sent both priests out of the country as soon as possible. Jalics went to the United States, and Yorio to Rome.

By 1978, the military dictatorship had defeated the guerrillas—the civil war was over. But the government-led terror had taken on a life of its own. The police and military felt free to seize, torture, and kill anyone, for any reason or no reason at all. Thousands of innocent people, with no connection to the rebels, were "disappeared."

The Mothers of the Plaza de Mayo

The Mothers of the Plaza de Mayo were women whose adult children were "disappeared"—kidnapped, tortured, and usually killed—during the military dictatorship in Argentina, 1976–83. They held their first rally in April 1977 in the main square of Buenos Aires. Wearing white scarves and carrying pictures of their children, the women walked silently every Thursday afternoon in front of the Casa Rosada, the presidential palace. They demanded information about their children, and they demanded justice for the government's human rights violations.

The government allowed the women to march, although they called the protesters *las locas,* "crazy women." But the Mothers' rallies, and their heart-rending stories, drew international attention, embarrassing the dictatorship. Some of the leaders of the Mothers of the Plaza de Mayo were themselves kidnapped and murdered by the government. Still, the protest marches continued.

After the Dirty War ended in 1983, the Mothers of the Plaza de Mayo continued to demand to know what had happened to their children. Eventually, many bodies of the "disappeared" were found and identified, and some of the guilty officials were brought to justice.

In the midst of the fear and anguish of the Dirty War, there were some spots of personal joy for Bergoglio. He kept in close touch with his family, especially his younger sister, María Elena. He was godfather to her first son. She named the baby Jorge, "in honor of my special brother." Years later, nephew Jorge would say that his famous uncle taught him his first swear words.

Jorge's brother Óscar had become a teacher, and

then an administrative clerk, and he had three children: Sebastián, Mauro, and Vanesa. Alberto had become an automotive parts salesman, and his children were Virna, Teseo Emanuel, and Ariadna. Marta had become a teacher with two sons, Pablo and José Luis Narvaja. José Luis followed his uncle's path in life, becoming a member of the Society of Jesus.

General Videla had come to power promising that his National Reorganization Process would restore Argentina to peace and prosperity. For the first few years after the coup, the middle class did enjoy prosperity, although it was based on money borrowed from foreign countries. And in 1978, when the soccer World Cup was held in Buenos Aires, Argentina won, creating a publicity boost for Videla's government. But gradually the junta's authority leaked away.

In spite of the dictatorship's extreme secrecy about the thousands of citizens who "disappeared," the international media found out about some of these stories and publicized them. Meanwhile, the economic boom did not last, partly because government officials stole public funds for their own use. Money meant for public projects, like a highway from Ezeiza airport to the center of Buenos Aires, was spirited off into private Swiss bank accounts. But before the project was abandoned, unfinished, the government had bulldozed many *villas miserias*, displacing hundreds of thousands of people.

By 1980, Argentina was suffering from severe recession and inflation. In April 1982, to distract from problems at home, the dictatorship invaded the Falkland Islands. Although the Falklands had been a British colony since 1841, they were only a few hundred miles off the coast of Argentina. In Argentina, the islands were stubbornly called by their Spanish name, the Islas Malvinas, and people felt that they ought to belong to Argentina. So the military government of Argentina hoped to boost their prestige by seizing the Falklands.

The Falklands were not actually valuable, in a practical way, to either the British or Argentina. The author Jorge Borges sarcastically called the Falklands War "two bald men fighting over a comb." Bergoglio, while he felt the islands rightly belonged to Argentina, thought the war was a tragic waste of the 649 Argentine soldiers who were killed. But at first, the people of Argentina did respond with patriotic enthusiasm.

The British, on the other hand, responded by sending a warship. Within ten weeks, Argentina had to surrender. Losing the war, together with the failing economy, was the final blow to the military government. In 1983, the most brutal dictatorship in the history of Argentina was forced to allow democratic elections. The Dirty War, as this period came to be called, was over.

But the suffering of more than fifteen thousand imprisoned, tortured, and murdered citizens would not be forgotten. The suffering of their relatives and friends would continue for decades. And the Jesuits of Argentina, including Jorge Bergoglio, would struggle to find their way back from these dark years.

CHAPTER 11
EXILE

JORGE BERGOGLIO'S SIX-YEAR TERM AS PROVIN-
cial for the Jesuits of Argentina had ended in December
1979, while Argentina was still in the grip of the military
dictatorship. Superior General Arrupe replaced Bergoglio with Father Andrés Swinnen, who had been novice
master, and he appointed Bergoglio rector of the Colegio
Máximo. Ernesto López Rosas became novice master.

These were comfortable changes for Bergoglio, since
the three men had known each other since the days when
they themselves were studying at the Colegio. In fact,

Swinnen had also shared Bergoglio's juniorate in Chile. Technically, Swinnen, as provincial, had authority over Bergoglio, as rector of the Colegio Máximo, but in practice, Swinnen continued Bergoglio's program for the province. Bergoglio, Swinnen, and López Rosas were all like-minded about what needed to be done in the province.

And Bergoglio, believing strongly in his mission to shape the training of Jesuits, was glad to be in direct charge of the Colegio. He took action in several ways to turn the Jesuit students away from politics and back to their calling as "God's Marines." He removed Marxist courses from the curriculum and replaced them with philosophy and theology courses on *teología del pueblo*, the theology of the people. He also promoted the teaching of Argentine history and literature, which he felt had been badly neglected.

In Bergoglio's view, discipline at the Colegio Máximo had gotten slack. The seminarians had been allowed to wear everyday clothes, and they felt free to leave the campus without notifying anyone. Bergoglio now required them to wear clerical collars, and to ask permission to go off campus.

Bergoglio also felt that Saint Ignatius Loyola's Spiritual Exercises had been neglected, and he made sure that the seminary students followed a routine of prayer several times a day. They were taught to use discernment, praying over each decision they made, because each decision had consequences. For their spiritual development, there were also talks and retreats, and each student met regularly with a spiritual director.

Rector Bergoglio expected the students at the Colegio Máximo to do physical work as well as study philosophy and theology. They had taken a vow of poverty, he reminded them, and the poor did manual labor. On one level, he thought the work was good for them; on another level, it was simply practical to open a farm with a vegetable garden and pigs, sheep, cows, and rabbits on the vacant grounds of the Colegio.

There were many mouths to feed at the seminary, to say nothing of the needy poor around them. The military dictatorship ended in 1983, with the election of Raúl Alfonsín of the Radical Party. But the dictatorship had burdened Argentina with a feeble economy, a huge national debt, and widespread unemployment. The economic slump would last for several years.

"I joined the Society of Jesus to study, not to look after pigs!" complained one student. But it was hard to argue when the rector himself worked in the pigpens. Bergoglio also did the laundry for the school, getting up at five thirty a.m. to throw clothes in the washing machines and hang them out to dry. He often cooked for the students. Paella was one of his specialties; stuffed suckling pig was another.

As when he was novice master, Bergoglio wanted his students to spend time with the poor. They must never forget that the main purpose of the Church, as Pope Paul VI had said, was to spread the Gospel. Jesuits, from the time of their founding by Ignatius Loyola, had always been missionaries. And all around the Colegio, in the slums of San Miguel, there were thousands of people living in poverty and outside the Church.

During the years he was in charge of the Colegio Máximo, 1979–85, Bergoglio built five churches to serve the people of the slums. His students were sent out Sunday mornings to round up children and bring them to Mass. He ordered the seminarians to find out what people needed—not poor people in general, but each individual, each family. If they were homeless, arrange for shelter. If they were hungry, bring them to the dining halls in the new churches. If they needed a bus ticket to a relative's funeral, the Colegio would find money to pay for it.

As much as anything, the people in the slums needed schooling and job training. Bergoglio opened schools, including skills workshops and adult education, next to the Colegio Máximo. He started children's summer camps at the seashore. Father Bergoglio himself loved to appear at a camp for the Sunday Mass and preach the homily, stepping down from the pulpit to stand in the congregation. He would get the children to cheer the saints and boo the devil as if they were at a soccer match.

Rector Bergoglio's idea in making his students serve the poor was not only for the benefit of the poor people, but also to put the students in touch with the faith of these people, the way they understood the Gospel. Bergoglio believed that this *teología del pueblo*, the theology of the people, was a truer understanding of Jesus's teaching than any abstract theology. The seminarians had much to learn, he felt, from God's holy faithful people. After they returned from their missions to the slums, he had them reflect on their experiences.

As an example, Bergoglio told the seminarians what he had learned from a poor woman named Marta. She was always asking for something for herself and her family, and it got annoying. One time, when she complained yet again that her family was hungry and cold, he lost patience. He told her to come back the next day, and he would try to help her.

"But Father," said Marta, "we're hungry *now*, and we're cold *now.*"

In that moment, Bergoglio felt that Christ was speaking to him through this woman. He found food for her. He went to his room, took a blanket off his bed, and gave it to her.

With his boundless energy and enthusiasm, and his gift for connecting with each person, Father Jorge Bergoglio was a hero to the working-class people of San Miguel. He was also a charismatic leader to his students, and during the early 1980s, the number of young men entering the seminary grew and grew. When he first took charge as rector of the Colegio Máximo in 1979, there were one hundred students; at the end of his term, in 1986, there were two hundred.

Bergoglio seemed like a kind of superman. Father Juan Carlos Scannone, who taught theology and philosophy at the Colegio Máximo, called him "an orchestra man." That was an Argentine term for someone who could do everything well, and all at once. "I remember one time he was typing up an article, then he went to put a wash on, and after that he received someone for spiritual advice. He was able to carry out a spiritual, mechanical, and manual task all at the same time and to the highest level."

But there were many Jesuits in Argentina who disagreed with Bergoglio's policies. And they resented the fact that he made decisions without consulting them. Even Father Swinnen, who thought Bergoglio made necessary changes, commented that "he handed himself a lot of authority; sometimes that was problematic."

During the twelve years that Jorge Bergoglio served as provincial, and then as rector of the Colegio Máximo, a split widened in the Jesuit province. There were the *bergoglianos*, who admired Bergoglio's leadership and were passionately loyal to him. And there were the *anti-bergoglianos*, who thought Bergoglio assumed too much authority. They were unhappy that Bergoglio, through his influence on Swinnen and López Rosas, continued to run the province even after his term as provincial was up.

The *anti-bergoglianos* were mainly older Jesuits, in particular a group called the Center for Social Research and Action (CIAS). They criticized Bergoglio for closing the base communities in the 1970s and for opposing the teaching of the socialist brand of liberation theology. Some felt that Bergoglio should have set a heroic example by speaking out against the dictatorship, as Father Mugica and Bishop Angelelli had done—and been murdered for it. They also pointed to the example of Archbishop Óscar Romero of San Salvador, assassinated during Mass on March 24, 1980, for defying the junta in El Salvador.

The Jesuits against Bergoglio thought that his encouragement of popular piety practices, such as venerating the statues of saints and making pilgrimages to shrines, was a step backward. They could see that he was devoted to improving the lives of the poor. But they thought he should be asking the political question: *Why* were they poor?

Bergoglio, on the other hand, considered many of the CIAS scholars detached from the real world. In his view, they spent their time developing theories about the causes of poverty, but avoided contact with actual poor people. He joked that their slogan was "All for the people but nothing with the people."

Bergoglio was criticized by Jesuits in other Latin American countries too. Father Fernando Montes, the Chilean Jesuit who knew Bergoglio from their days as seminarians, was now provincial of Chile. Montes spoke out openly for human rights and against the military dictatorship of General Augusto Pinochet. He believed that the CIAS in Argentina was doing important work for human rights, and he thought Bergoglio should have been more supportive of them.

In Rome, Superior General Arrupe had always firmly backed Bergoglio's leadership. But he became ill and was replaced in 1983, and then Bergoglio's opponents in Argentina felt freer to speak up. They complained to the new superior general of the Jesuits, Peter-Hans Kolvenbach.

Then in 1986, the mounting criticisms came to a head. As Jorge Bergoglio's six years as rector of the Colegio Máximo ended, a devastating accusation from the time of the Dirty War was brought against him. President Alfonsín had ordered an investigation into the "disappearances," and many victims of the military dictatorship began to speak up.

Bergoglio's accuser was Emilio Mignone, in his book *Witness to the Truth: The Complicity of Church and Dictatorship in Argentina, 1976–1983*. During the rule of the junta, Mignone's daughter Mónica, a teacher in the same *villa miseria* as Yorio and Jalics, had been kidnapped and "disappeared." Mignone had gone from bishop to bishop, desperate to find his daughter, but no one in the Church could help him.

Mignone had come to believe that the whole Church in Argentina, including Bergoglio, had collaborated with the military dictatorship. He wrote that Bergoglio had actually betrayed Franz Jalics and Orlando Yorio, the slum priests who disobeyed his orders to leave their base community. According to Mignone, Bergoglio had given a "green light" for them to be seized by the security forces. Bergoglio and other conservative priests, Mignone implied, hoped that the dictatorship would wipe out the dangerous doctrine of Marxist liberation theology as well as the rebels.

At the time Mignone's book came out, Bergoglio did not defend himself. Perhaps he thought that the shocking accusation was obviously untrue. Or that it was the result of years of anguished brooding by the father of a murdered daughter, and that it would be unkind to argue.

In truth, some in the Church of Argentina actually had collaborated with the dictatorship. Two conservative bishops in particular—Adolfo Tortolo, archbishop of Paraná, and Victorio Bonamín, bishop to military chaplains—had approved of and aided the military government's persecution of leftists. Some priests and nuns had even helped with kidnappings, torture, and murder. The archbishop of Buenos Aires, Cardinal Aramburu, had denied that Bishop Angelelli's death in 1976 was a murder, and he had refused many times to help the parents of the disappeared.

In 1986 the Jesuit superior general, Kolvenbach, concluded that Jorge Bergoglio's influence in the Argentina province had become too divisive. Although for years Bergoglio had been so effective in attracting novices to the Society of Jesus, during the 1980s many Jesuits in Argentina—more than one hundred—had left the order. With the goal of reuniting the province, Kolvenbach chose Father Victor Zorzín, favored by the CIAS Jesuits, as the new provincial.

Once Zorzín took over, he thought it best to get Jorge Bergoglio out of Argentina for the time being. In May he sent him to Frankfurt, Germany, for two years to work on his PhD thesis.

It must have been difficult for Bergoglio, after running the Jesuit province of Argentina for twelve years, to suddenly be thousands of miles from home with no one to oversee but himself. In Germany Bergoglio dutifully applied himself to research, but he was homesick and unhappy. In the evenings, he took walks in the cemetery, from which he could see planes taking off from Frankfurt Airport. A friend asked him what he was doing, and Bergoglio answered, "I'm waving to the planes bound for Argentina."

Bergoglio was now fifty years old, wondering what further mission God had for him. After several months in Germany, he went on a pilgrimage to Augsburg, to a Jesuit church named St. Peter am Perlach. In the church, he was drawn to a painting of the Virgin Mary, showing her untying knots in an endless ribbon. Bergoglio must have felt that his own life was full of knots, because the painting held special meaning for him. He prayed there for hours.

Bergoglio left the church in Augsburg feeling sure that he was meant to return home. Apparently the leadership of the province had not actually *ordered* him to stay in Germany for two years, or he would have obeyed. Instead, he showed up in Buenos Aires in December 1986. He never finished his PhD thesis.

Zorzín, the provincial, still didn't know what to do with Bergoglio. He was given a room and a part-time teaching job at the secondary school Colegio del Salvador, where he had taught twenty years ago. Bergoglio's friend Ernesto López Rosas was the current rector of the Colegio Máximo, and he invited him to teach a once-a-week course on pastoral theology.

Bergoglio was still popular among many of the Jesuits in Argentina, especially the younger ones who had gone through their years of training under his guidance. In March 1987, they elected him procurator of the province. The procurator's job was to report on the state of his province to the superior general in Rome, as well as to a meeting of the procurators from all the provinces.

Perhaps Bergoglio had had this procurator's mission in mind when he returned early from Germany. In September 1987 he flew to Rome for the meeting of Jesuit procurators. In the report he presented, he must have had much to criticize about the province of Argentina, where all the reforms he had made were being wiped out. However, Superior General Kolvenbach, who regarded Bergoglio as the source of the division among Argentine Jesuits, was not open to listening.

And over the next two years, the division continued to grow. Bergoglio had no official authority over the province of Argentina, but nevertheless many Jesuits looked to him for guidance. Zorzín, the Argentine provincial, blamed Bergoglio for stirring up discontent.

In April 1987 the Catholics of Argentina reveled in a new event: World Youth Day was held in Buenos Aires. World Youth Day is an international event begun by Pope John Paul II in 1985 and held every two or three years in different countries. The idea was to bring together Catholic young people of all cultures, to appreciate their diversity and to celebrate their unity in the Church.

On the Avenida de Mayo, Pope John Paul II celebrated Mass for a congregation of about one million. Jorge Bergoglio was one of the hundreds of priests who assisted at the Mass, hearing confessions and handing out Communion bread. He had the chance to meet the pope, briefly.

John Paul II had been elected pope in 1978, when Jorge Bergoglio was still the Jesuit provincial. This pope had a vigorous, magnetic personality, and he became immensely popular worldwide. The media liked to call him a "rock star."

However, his views on Catholic theology were more conservative than those of John XXIII or Paul VI. Having lived in Poland through the years of oppression by Soviet Russia, he was firmly anticommunist. He did all he could to discourage the Marxist brand of liberation theology in Latin America.

Early in 1990, Provincial Zorzín decided that the solution to the discord among the Jesuits was to remove Bergoglio and his followers. He asked Father López Rosas, the rector at the Colegio Máximo, to remove Bergoglio from his teaching position and from his room at the Colegio. It must have been a shock, since López Rosas was a friend, and the Colegio had been Bergoglio's home for the last twenty-five years.

Bergoglio's closest followers were sent abroad. Bergoglio himself was sent to Córdoba, safely hundreds of miles away from the Jesuit novices and seminarians and from the provincial office. Supposedly he was there for the purpose of further work on his PhD thesis at the University of Córdoba. But most of his friends were forbidden to contact him, and his letters and telephone calls were censored.

The only real responsibility Bergoglio was given in Córdoba was the job of hearing confessions. The people coming to him for confession were students and teachers

A drawing of the magnificent dome of St. Peter's Basilica in Vatican City, Rome, circa 1700.

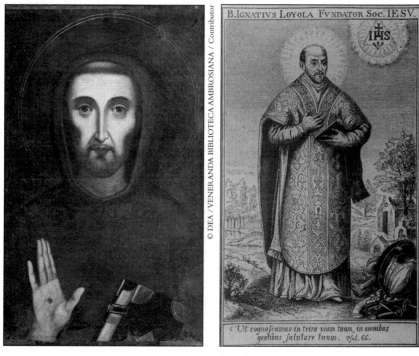

Saint Francis of Assisi, founder of the Franciscan Order.

Saint Ignatius of Loyola (1491–1556), founder of the Society of Jesus, whose story was inspirational to Jorge Bergoglio.

Jorge Bergoglio (standing, second from left) with his family. His sister Maria is in the white dress, on the far left.

Jorge Bergoglio's bedroom at the Colegio Máximo, San Miguel, Buenos Aires, Argentina, where he studied for the priesthood.

Pope John XXIII at the opening of the Second Vatican Council at St. Peter's Basilica in Vatican City, 1962. The members were brought together to decide how the Catholic Church should relate to the modern world.

December 1965: Closing ceremony of the Second Vatican Council in December 1965.

President of Argentina Juan Perón and his wife, Eva Perón, marking the anniversary of the Peronist movement in October 1950.

Jorge Rafael Videla (left), dictator of Argentina, and Alfredo Stroessner (right), dictator of Paraguay, at a military parade in Asuncion, Paraguay, in April 1977.

Argentines celebrate as new president Raul Alfonsin takes office, marking the end of seven years of harsh military rule.

Pope John Paul II meets with the exiled spiritual leader of Tibet, the Dalai Lama, in Vatican City in 1982.

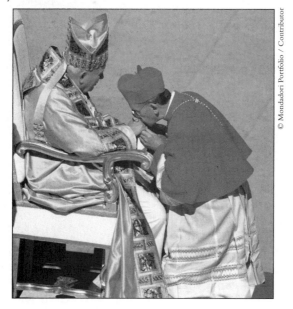

Pope John Paul II (seated) makes Bergoglio a cardinal in Vatican City, February 21, 2001.

On March 13, 2013, after being elected the 266th pope, Francis addresses the crowds from the balcony of St. Peter's Basilica.

On March 19, 2013, hundreds of thousands gather in St. Peter's Square for Pope Francis's inauguration Mass.

Pope Francis in his popemobile, riding through New York City's Central Park on September 25, 2015.

President Barack Obama greets Pope Francis on his arrival at Joint Base Andrews, September 22, 2015. This was the pope's first visit to the United States.

On July 29, 2016, Pope Francis visits Auschwitz, the Nazi death camp, to meet with Holocaust survivors and pray for the 1.1 million victims murdered here during World War II.

In his weekly audience in St. Peter's Square, Pope Francis meets with victims of war, April 5, 2017.

at the University of Córdoba, as well as people from the slums around the city, where there were too few priests for too many people. For Bergoglio, who had led the Jesuits of Argentina as novice master, provincial, and rector, it was a humbling comedown.

Of course, Bergoglio had always known that the Jesuit way was not to move a leader toward ever-greater power and glory. When a Jesuit's term in a leadership position was over, he was supposed to step into the background. Also, Bergoglio had taken a vow of obedience—not to obey only if he agreed with his leader's decisions, but simply to *obey*. He had expected this kind of obedience from Franz Jalics and Orlando Yorio, and he had been deeply troubled when they defied his orders. Now it was his turn to obey.

Jesuit Obedience

The first vows a Jesuit novice takes are for poverty, chastity, and *obedience*. From day one of the novitiate, Jesuits-in-training are pledged to obey the novice master. The founder of the Society of Jesus, Ignatius Loyola, was originally a soldier, and he expected militarylike discipline and obedience from the men who joined the order. Jesuits were to be available to go anywhere and do anything for the greater glory of God.

Unless they were missionaries out in the field, Jesuits lived in communities, in Jesuit residences. The communities were grouped into a province, supervised by a provincial general. The provinces were organized into ten regions—usually a large part of a continent—governed by a regional assistant. And the superior general, based in Rome, was the commander for all the Jesuits in the world. Only the pope had higher authority over the Jesuits than the superior general.

Although at each level the leader commanded obedience from the Jesuits in his charge, the posts were not permanent. A province leader served for six years, and then it was time for another Jesuit to take the reins. The superior general, too, served for a term of only six years. The exception to this rule was the pope himself, but he was usually not a Jesuit.

Bergoglio had never felt so alone as during his two years in Córdoba. He was a person who needed to be with other people. One of the reasons he had become a Jesuit, rather than a parish priest, was that the Jesuits lived in communities. Yet in Córdoba, he could not take comfort from other people. Although he lived in the main residence, he kept to himself.

Bergoglio prayed more than ever; he listened to

confessions. He had no idea of where his life could go now. "I lived a time of great interior crisis," he told an interviewer years later. Perhaps he even wondered if he had been mistaken about the revelation he experienced four years ago, kneeling in the German church before Mary, Untier of Knots.

Centuries ago Ignatius Loyola had described the spiritual state Bergoglio was in as "desolation." His usual cheerfulness and energy were gone, and he hardly slept or ate. The other Jesuits in the residence became worried, and they brought a doctor to see him. The theologian Father Scannone, his friend and former teacher, came to visit, and he was also worried. He could tell by the look on Bergoglio's face that he was "going through a dark night."

The Jesuits' doctor gave Bergoglio a medal of the Virgin of Guadalupe from Mexico, thinking that it might comfort him. In fact, Jorge Bergoglio, known by some as the inscrutable "Mona Lisa," was deeply touched. He put the chain around his neck with tears in his eyes.

Part of the reason for Bergoglio's despair must have been that his reforms in the Jesuit province were still being reversed. At the Colegio Máximo, the discipline he had imposed was dropped. Students were not required to work on the farm, or to go out into the slums on Sundays and bring children into the new churches. Bergoglio's whole project of enabling the seminarians, the priests, and the poor people living around them to experience the Gospel together was dissolved.

Ironically, Bergoglio's absence did not seem to be helping the Jesuits heal their divisions or increase their membership. The number of novices entering the order dropped, and the number of Jesuits quitting the order grew.

Bergoglio had worked so hard for the last fifteen years, with confidence that he was doing God's will. If all he had accomplished could be wiped out so quickly, what did that mean? Maybe it meant that he had been following his own will, rather than God's. Years later, he would see this period of desolation as an opportunity for his spiritual growth. As he put it, sometimes spiritual needs "get put aside until you slip on a banana peel and fall."

During the many hours Bergoglio spent in prayer and discernment, he concluded that it was not that he had made the wrong decisions. Rather, he had gone about making decisions the wrong *way*. He had not respected other Jesuits' views or included them in the process. "It was my authoritarian way of making decisions that created problems," he said later.

All of Jorge Bergoglio's extraordinary intelligence, energy, devotion, and charisma—his brilliant "orchestra man" act—was no help to him now. He continued to pray, he suffered silently, and he waited for God to act.

Although Bergoglio felt alone, he was not forgotten. Outside the Jesuit order, many leaders in the Church, in Argentina and elsewhere, had a high opinion of Bergoglio's gifts and wanted to make use of them. One such leader was Antonio Quarracino, archbishop of Buenos Aires.

CHAPTER 12

THE BISHOP OF THE SLUMS

UBALDO CALABRESI, THE POPE'S NUNCIO, OR ambassador, to Argentina, had a big surprise for Jorge Bergoglio. But he didn't say so. He merely asked Bergoglio to meet him at the Córdoba airport to talk for a few hours between flights. Calabresi had often called Bergoglio on the phone to consult with him about the affairs of the province, so Bergoglio didn't expect anything unusual from this meeting in May 1992. But as Calabresi left to board his plane, he said, "Ah, one last thing, you've been named auxiliary bishop of Buenos Aires."

Bergoglio's mind went blank, as he told it later. "Whenever something really unexpected happens, whether good or bad, my mind always goes blank." This certainly qualified as "really unexpected." Just like that, he was plucked out of lonely exile in Córdoba and set down in the busy life of an urban bishop.

When Jorge Bergoglio joined the Society of Jesus, he had vowed that he would never seek to obtain a high office in the Church. All Jesuits make a commitment not to give in to the temptation of ambition for their own advancement. Saint Ignatius had called such ambition "the mother of all evils in any community or congregation." The idea was that a high position in the Church always brought wealth and power, and temptations to the sins of pride and self-will.

However, Jesuits also vow obedience—obedience, above all, to the pope—and that vow comes first. John Paul II had decided that Bergoglio should serve the Church as a bishop in Buenos Aires. As a Jesuit, Bergoglio could not disobey the pope. But as a result of his obedience, he would not be living the life of a Jesuit anymore. His allegiance would now be to his archbishop, rather than to his provincial.

Cardinal Antonio Quarracino, archbishop of Buenos Aires since July 1990, was the force behind Jorge Bergoglio's big surprise. He had specifically asked the pope to appoint Bergoglio as one of his six auxiliary, or assistant, bishops. For some years, Quarracino had been planning to bring Bergoglio onto his team when he had a chance.

Early in 1990, when Quarracino was still archbishop of La Plata, he had invited Bergoglio to lead retreats for his clergy, and he was impressed with Bergoglio's spirituality and leadership. He also admired what Bergoglio had accomplished in his mission to the poor neighborhoods of San Miguel, when he was rector of the Colegio Máximo. That was the kind of renewal Quarracino wanted Bergoglio to bring to the archdiocese of Buenos Aires.

On June 27, 1992, at the age of fifty-five, Bergoglio was ordained a bishop. He chose a motto for himself: *Miserando atque eligendo*. The Latin can be translated as, "And looking at him mercifully, he chose him." It refers to the story, in the Gospel according to Matthew, about Jesus picking Matthew, a hated tax collector, to be his disciple. Bergoglio's point was that he did not consider himself any worthier than Matthew had been. But he believed that Jesus was looking at him, also, with the eyes of mercy, and choosing him to do this work.

After the ordination ceremony, crowds of poor people came up to Bishop Bergoglio to congratulate him. Many of them were from San Miguel, from the poor parishes around the Colegio Máximo. He had a card to give each one of them—a card with a picture of Mary, Untier of Knots. Bergoglio had brought stacks of the picture, with its special meaning for him, from Germany.

Quarracino put Bergoglio in charge of the Flores section of Buenos Aires, the poorest part of the city. His rooms and office were in the clergy retirement house, not far from San José de Flores, the church where he had first heard a call to the priesthood. This was Jorge Bergoglio's old neighborhood, although none of his family lived there anymore. But one beloved person from Bergoglio's childhood was still nearby: Dolores Tortolo, at the Sisters of Mercy. Now it would be easier to visit her at the convent.

Bergoglio was also not far from the stadium where the San Lorenzo soccer team played. If he was too busy with his bishop's duties to be in the stands, he listened to the games on the radio while he worked at his desk. One patient he visited during his hospital rounds complained that the bishop gave bad soccer-bet tips. "Father Bergoglio was always sure that San Lorenzo would win! And they always lost."

By the time Bergoglio became an auxiliary bishop in Buenos Aires, Carlos Menem had been the president of Argentina for several years. Shortly after his election in 1989, Menem declared amnesty for crimes committed during the Dirty War. He freed the prisoners who had been convicted of such crimes, including the leaders of the dictatorship and hundreds of officers. As for Menem's economic policies, he favored private business and foreign investors. At first it seemed that he could stabilize the shaky economy of Argentina. He was elected to a second term in 1994.

The rich and the middle class did enjoy prosperity during these years. But at the same time, Menem's policies threw many people, especially government employees, out of work. The poor became poorer, and the number of people living in poverty grew. In Buenos Aires and other cities, the *villas miserias* also grew and grew.

The rural provinces were poor, with no chance for work and no health services, so poor people moved to the city. But they could not afford to pay rent in Buenos

Aires, so they built shacks on empty land from shoddy bricks, scrap lumber, and cardboard. A roof might be corrugated sheet metal, weighted down with rocks. The slums sprang up along railroad tracks, beside the city dump, and on the banks of the polluted rivers. These *villas* lacked water, sanitation, and electricity. Not much had changed for the poorest of the poor, except that there were many more of them.

Menem had promised to shrink Argentina's debt, but actually his government borrowed from foreign banks until the international debt ballooned from $62 billion to $127 billion. And corruption spread. Menem appointed his relatives to government positions and indulged himself in a luxurious lifestyle. Foreign investors found that they could not do business in Argentina without paying large bribes. Even the Catholic Church in Buenos Aires, as Bergoglio would find out, was entangled in Menem's political corruption.

As a new auxiliary bishop, Bergoglio surprised the priests and people of Flores with his personal care for them. Most bishops run their diocese from their offices, but Bergoglio spent his time in the streets. He visited each parish priest, shared a gourd of maté, and took the time to get to know him. "He came to see you and he listened," said one priest gratefully.

Whatever the problems in each parish, Bergoglio personally saw to it that they were solved quickly. If the priest needed funds for a project, Bergoglio found the money. He had a fatherlike concern for his priests, visiting them when they were sick, sometimes even cooking for them.

In one case, a young priest came to believe that he had been mistaken to think he had a call to the priesthood. Bergoglio, instead of rejecting him, helped him discern the right decision. As the young man left the priesthood, Bergoglio helped him get a job and even gave him three years' worth of rent money.

Bishop Bergoglio always asked his priests about the time they spent in prayer. Without prayer, he said, a priest was only a social worker. Prayer had brought him through his dark period in Córdoba, making him more intensely aware of his dependence on God. "If the Lord does not help in this work of assisting the People of God to go forward," he explained later, "it can't be done." And Bergoglio believed that they all needed one another's prayers. Whoever he talked with, he asked that person to pray for him.

The priests and the people of Flores noticed that their

new bishop did not arrive in their neighborhoods in a car with a chauffeur. Instead he traveled on the subway and on buses. Also, he had no secretary to screen his phone calls. You could call him directly, any time after six o'clock in the morning.

By December 1993, Cardinal Quarracino must have been pleased that he'd made the extra effort to get Jorge Bergoglio appointed a bishop. He had seen Bishop Bergoglio in action, and he had heard many glowing reports. "Do you know who the best-loved auxiliary bishop among the young clerics of Buenos Aires is?" he remarked to Father Juan Carlos Scannone. "Bergoglio!"

Among the Jesuits, there were many who blamed Bergoglio for the troubles in their order, and they were still very angry with him. But he was no longer under their jurisdiction.

Quarracino was so satisfied with Bishop Bergoglio's work that he appointed him vicar-general of the whole archdiocese of Buenos Aires. That meant that Bergoglio was the cardinal's right-hand man. More and more, Bergoglio was the one who managed the archdiocese.

One serious issue that Bergoglio had to manage was

corruption. The Church in Argentina had become deeply entangled with the government of Carlos Menem. The government secretly gave the Church large sums of money, and the Church went along with the government's policies.

This arrangement became crystal clear to Bergoglio when he had a visit from two particular officials. They said they wanted to donate $400,000 in aid for the slums of Buenos Aires. The actual deal, it came out, was that they would give him $200,000 under the table—but he would need to sign a receipt for $400,000. They would keep the other $200,000 for themselves.

Bergoglio immediately understood that this kind of deal between the Church and the Menem government must have been going on for some time. He told them that any large donation to the archdiocese had to go through regular bank channels. That was the last he saw of those two officials.

In spite of his high position in Buenos Aires, Bergoglio made a point of not drawing attention to himself. With his humble behavior, Bergoglio set an example for all the priests and people of Buenos Aires. And it helped him control any pride he might feel.

As Bergoglio had learned in his Jesuit training, the best way to combat a temptation was to deliberately go in the other direction. If you are tempted to pray less, pray twice as much. If you are tempted to take pride in your talents and accomplishments, sit down in the back row and keep quiet.

Even after all his training and experience, Bergoglio still sometimes caught himself in a state of self-pride. One day Archbishop Quarracino was out of town and Bergoglio was in charge of the diocese of Buenos Aires. He was feeling especially pleased with his ability to "play Tarzan," as he put it.

He was swinging from task to task without missing a beat, handling each task superbly. At two o'clock, according to his tight schedule, he had to leave his office for the train station. He would catch the train to Castelar, west of Buenos Aires, where he was to give Spiritual Exercises to a group of nuns.

But first, Bergoglio ducked into the nearby cathedral to say a quick prayer. On his way out, he met a young man who seemed mentally disturbed—perhaps on medication. The young man asked Bergoglio to hear his confession.

Bergoglio told him briskly that another priest would have to hear his confession, "because I've got something to do." Bergoglio knew that actually the cathedral priest wouldn't be in until four o'clock. But he thought the young man, in his medicated state, might not notice.

Then, as Bergoglio strode away to catch his train, he was overcome with shame. What important "something" could be more important than hearing a confession? How could he, who had experienced intimacy with God during confession, refuse anyone else? He turned back and told the young man, "The father is going to be late; I will hear you confess."

When Bergoglio finally reached the train station, it turned out that the train to Castelar was half an hour late, and so he caught it after all.

Bergoglio was still decisive, but he had changed his style of leadership. When he was provincial of the Jesuits, he tended to make decisions by himself. In contrast, as overseer of the archdiocese, he consulted with the auxiliary bishops and with the council of priests first, and then he made the decisions.

With unfaltering energy, Bergoglio visited the *villas miserias* of the city and encouraged the "slum priests." One of the best known and loved was Father José María di

Paola, known as "Padre Pepe." His parish, Villa 21, had a large number of immigrants from Paraguay. They were descendants of the Guaraní tribes that the Jesuit missionaries had introduced to Christianity centuries ago.

In 1997, when Father di Paola proposed to bring an icon of the Virgin of Caacupé from Paraguay to Villa 21, Bergoglio was glad to give him the money for the project. The Virgin of Caacupé, a patron saint of Paraguay, was originally an image carved by a Guaraní Indian. Bergoglio agreed with di Paola that the symbolism of the icon would draw the people of the *villa* together and help them take pride in their community.

When the icon arrived in Buenos Aires, Bergoglio held a special Mass of celebration at the Catedral Metropolitano, the cathedral of Buenos Aires. Then there was a grand procession from the cathedral, on the Plaza de Mayo, to the alleys of Villa 21. Father di Paola didn't see Bergoglio in the procession, and he assumed that the bishop had stayed at the cathedral. But then someone spotted Bishop Bergoglio walking at the back of the line—not in his festival robes, but wearing a poncho and quietly praying the rosary. By his actions, he was saying, *What is truly important here is the people of this parish and their devotion to Mary, Mother of Jesus.*

• • •

Bishop Bergoglio demonstrated his support for the poor even against the most powerful politicians. In January 1996 the city government of Buenos Aires planned to bulldoze a large part of Villa 31 in order to construct a new freeway. But Father Carlos Mugica had worked in this slum. He had been murdered here in 1974, when Isabel Perón was president, by a right-wing death squad. Mugica was still remembered as a hero who had given his life for the people of the slums, his picture tacked up on the walls of shacks as if he were a saint.

The idea of bulldozing the place where Mugica had lived out his mission was outrageous to the people of the *villas*. All the slum priests, with Bergoglio's backing, went on a hunger strike in protest. They set up tents in the way of the bulldozers, and they stayed there, fasting, for two weeks.

The mayor of Buenos Aires, Jorge Dominguez, was furious, and so was President Menem. But with reporters and TV crews publicizing the hunger strike, they were afraid to order the police to drag off the protesters. Bergoglio visited the tents often to show his support, and he even persuaded Cardinal Quarracino to appear.

The message was clear: the whole Church stood with the poor. Bergoglio finally brokered a deal in which the priests called off the strike, and the government put the freeway somewhere else.

Cardinal Quarracino's health was failing, and he was determined to make sure that Bergoglio would be appointed archbishop of Buenos Aires after him. This would not be easy, because Bergoglio had made an enemy of Menem by siding with the people of the *villas* against the government, and by refusing to go along with the usual corruption. Under Argentine law, President Menem had the right to veto a nomination. Also, other powerful people in Argentina and at the Vatican favored one of the other bishops of Buenos Aires, Héctor Aguer.

However, Quarracino once again made use of his close friendship with Pope John Paul II. He got the pope to sign a letter appointing Bergoglio as coadjutor archbishop, Quarracino's successor. With the pope's blessing, Bergoglio would replace Quarracino, and no other permission was needed.

Bergoglio, meanwhile, only knew the obstacles Quarracino would face in trying to make him coadjutor archbishop. He assumed that the archbishop would instead appoint him bishop of another diocese. Bergoglio asked Quarracino to let him go back to being an auxiliary bishop in Buenos Aires instead. "I come from Buenos Aires, and outside that city I'm incapable of doing anything," he explained.

Once more, Nuncio Ubaldo Calabresi arrived from Rome to spring a surprise on Bergoglio. Calabresi invited Bergoglio out to lunch. At the end of the meal, when Bergoglio was about to thank the nuncio and say good-bye, the waiter brought out cake and sparkling wine.

Bergoglio thought it must be Calabresi's birthday, and he started to congratulate him. "The fact is," said Calabresi with a gleeful smile, "you're the new coadjutor bishop of Buenos Aires." As before, Jorge Bergoglio's mind went blank, and he was speechless.

On February 28, 1998, Quarracino died, and Jorge Bergoglio became archbishop of Buenos Aires. But Bergoglio was a very different kind of archbishop. Quarracino had enjoyed all the perks of his position: the splendid robes, the palatial archbishop's residence in a wealthy suburb, a limousine with a chauffeur. He liked mingling in high society, attending lavish dinner parties, and receiving the attention of the media. But Bergoglio intended to follow Pope Paul VI's recommendation, at the end of the Second Vatican Council, that all Catholic clergy should be "poor, simple, humble, and lovable."

As the new archbishop, Bergoglio could have gained a great deal of publicity right away. But he turned down all requests from the media for interviews. And he didn't change his way of living at all. He didn't see any need for a chauffeur—he was a good driver himself, and he usually took public transportation anyway. However, he didn't want to put the archbishop's driver out of work, so he found him another job.

Archbishop Bergoglio refused to live in the archbishop's princely residence. He chose two small rooms for himself in the archdiocesan office building, next to the cathedral on the Plaza de Mayo. In his bedroom he hung the crucifix that had belonged to Grandmother Rosa and Grandfather Giovanni. He also put up a poster of the San Lorenzo soccer team, signed by all the players.

Bergoglio realized he would need archbishop's clothes, the black tunics with purple piping, for official occasions. But instead of ordering new ones, he had Quarracino's tunics taken in to fit him. And most of the time, he wore a plain black priest's suit. When he traveled around the city as usual, by bus or subway, most people had no idea who he was.

Unlike Quarracino, Bergoglio turned down invitations to dinner, because late-night events would interfere with his routine. He needed to go to bed by ten p.m. in order to get up at four a.m. and spend an hour or so in prayer. During this time, he considered the decisions he had to make that day, using Saint Ignatius's method of spiritual discernment.

At seven o'clock Archbishop Bergoglio said Mass, then brewed his own maté. He ate a light breakfast while he read the newspapers. A newsstand on the Plaza de Mayo delivered the papers every morning.

By eight thirty, Bergoglio had left his private rooms on the third floor and arrived in his office in the same building. That office, a simple room with a desk and three chairs, was no more luxurious than his living quarters. On his desk he kept three pictures: Saint Joseph, Saint Thérèse of Lisieux, and Mary, Untier of Knots.

The morning was filled with meetings and phone calls, which Bergoglio placed himself. After a light lunch and a short nap, he spent the afternoon in more archdiocesan business. He often ended his workday with visits to parishes, especially the poorer ones. Then, after a simple supper—sometimes pasta that he cooked for himself in his little kitchen—he ended the day in prayer, as he had begun. If he was so tired that he dozed off in front of the altar, he didn't reproach himself, because he felt that he was in God's hands.

Bergoglio did accept an invitation, soon after he became archbishop, to dinner at the Metropolitan Seminary. After the meal, the rector of the seminary invited him to speak to the students. Bergoglio stood up to speak. They all waited for some words of wisdom to the priests-in-training from His Excellency, the head of the Church in Buenos Aires.

What Bergoglio said was, "I'll wash the plates tonight." And he did.

Always at the forefront of Jorge Bergoglio's mind was that he was not meant to be served—he was meant to serve others. Jesus had set this example for his disciples on the night before his crucifixion. Jesus, their leader and teacher, had washed their feet. And he had told the disciples to do the same for others.

On Holy Thursday 1998, instead of celebrating the Mass of the Last Supper at the cathedral, Bergoglio arranged to say Mass at a hospital. The chaplain warned him that most of the patients had HIV-AIDS, and some of them were drug dealers and prostitutes. But Bergoglio, as he always insisted to the priests under his direction, believed that when you're a priest, you're a priest for everyone. He gave them Communion and washed their feet, both men and women. "The patients were totally overwhelmed," the chaplain remembered.

Although Cardinal Quarracino had placed Jorge Bergoglio in a position where he could do a great deal of good, he had also left Bergoglio with a financial mess. Just before Quarracino died, a major corruption scandal, involving the Church and President Menem's government, had come to light. It turned out that a major Argentine bank, the Banco de Credito Provincial (BCP), had borrowed $10 million, using the cardinal's name. Actually, the bank's owners, the Trusso family, had used the money to prop the bank up. And Quarracino's own secretary had assisted in this scheme, forging the archbishop's signature.

Faced with this disaster, Bergoglio acted quickly and

decisively. He brought in independent accountants to examine the records, and he provided the justice system with the paperwork to prosecute the criminals. To prevent any future corrupt deals, Bergoglio transferred the archdiocese's funds to banks in which they had no shares. In 1999, a new government, led by President Fernando de la Rúa, took office in Argentina.

During Bergoglio's years as archbishop, there was a healing of an old wound. Franz Jalics, one of the slum priests kidnapped and tortured during the Dirty War, had spent many years believing that his provincial had betrayed him and Orlando Yorio to the dictatorship. But finally it came out that the military had actually gotten Jalics's and Yorio's names from a lay teacher, under torture. Sadly, Yorio died in 2000 still blaming Bergoglio for his kidnapping.

Jalics, now a retreat leader, and Bergoglio, now an archbishop, met in Germany in 2001. It had been more than twenty years since Jalics had been seized by the dictatorship and thrown into a secret prison, and since Bergoglio had frantically labored to have him freed. The two Jesuit priests celebrated Mass together—and then they hugged each other, crying.

CHAPTER 13

ENEMIES OF THE PEOPLE

JORGE BERGOGLIO DID NOT ENJOY GOING TO ROME.
It was part of his job as an archbishop to make journeys
to the Vatican from time to time, but he would have
preferred to stay in Buenos Aires. He was happiest with
the people of the *villas*, in the middle of a throng at a
religious fiesta, or visiting a family in their corrugated
metal shack.

Archbishop Bergoglio's trips to the Vatican, the center
of the worldwide Catholic Church, brought out his serious side. He deeply admired and respected John Paul II,

but the Vatican, the administration of the entire Roman Catholic Church, was another matter. The walled papal state of Vatican City, full of clergy struggling to gain or showing off their power, privilege, and prestige, faced him with the "spiritual worldliness" that needed reforming in the Church. But at the beginning of 2001, Pope John Paul II summoned Bergoglio to Rome, to be made a cardinal, and there was no way to avoid this trip.

Of course, being named a cardinal was a high honor, not only for Bergoglio, but also for his country, Argentina. Cardinals advised the pope on church matters, and when a pope died, they chose the new pope. At the end of 2000, there were fewer than one hundred cardinals in the world, most of them from Italy.

Pope John Paul II was creating forty-four new cardinals. Ten of them, including Cláudio Hummes of São Paulo, Brazil, and Jorge Bergoglio, were from Latin America. This seemed fitting, since of the more than one billion Catholics in the world, almost half of them lived in Central and South America. There were rumors that the next pope would be Latin American.

Many of Bergoglio's friends and supporters would have liked to go to Rome for the ceremony, but Bergoglio asked them not to. Instead he asked them to give to the poor the money they would have spent on the trip. He himself flew coach class. His sister María Elena also flew from Buenos Aires for the event.

Cardinals visiting Rome often stayed in large hotels, but Bergoglio chose a modest guesthouse for clergy, Domus Internationalis Paulus VI. On the day of the ceremony, he put on the same black orthopedic shoes he wore for walking in the *villas miserias* of Buenos Aires. Rather than taking a limousine or even a taxi, he walked from his lodgings to the Vatican. His cardinal's scarlet vestments were secondhand, formerly Quarracino's. Bergoglio covered them with a black coat so as not to attract attention on the streets.

At St. Peter's Square, Pope John Paul II, in splendid gold vestments, sat on a throne to receive each new cardinal one by one. John Paul II had been a fit and vigorous man for most of his twenty-five-year papacy. In 1981 he had been badly wounded in an assassination attempt, but he recovered.

But now the pope was eighty. With advancing Parkinson's disease, he struggled to walk and speak. Bergoglio in his turn knelt in front of the pope and received his biretta (cardinal's scarlet hat) and gold ring. He was deeply moved by the pope's fierce dedication to his office.

On this trip to Italy, Jorge Bergoglio took the opportunity to get out of Rome and visit a place he had never been—but where he felt strangely at home. He and his sister traveled to the Piedmont region in northwestern Italy. The beautiful countryside of vineyard-covered hills was even more beautiful to them because it was the homeland of their ancestors.

They met relatives they had never seen—a great-uncle, uncles, cousins. Bergoglio chatted easily with them in the Piedmontese dialect, just as he used to talk with his grandparents. He and María Elena stopped in Turin, where Grandma Rosa and Grandfather Giovanni had run their coffee shop, and visited the town of Portacomaro, where their father, Mario, had spent his childhood.

Returning to Argentina, Bergoglio was still archbishop of Buenos Aires, but now he had an additional responsibility. As a cardinal, he would be one of those to vote when it was time to elect the next pope. And that time seemed likely to come soon, considering John Paul II's ill health.

• • •

In 2001, the same year that Jorge Bergoglio became a cardinal, the Vatican began a lengthy investigation into an ongoing scandal: thousands of accusations that Catholic priests had sexually abused children, and that bishops had protected the abusers. Ever since the 1980s, a growing number of people had stepped forward to tell their appalling stories. It was bad enough that children had been abused by priests, and worse that some higher authorities in the Church, including bishops, had refused to believe them. Worst of all, many abusive priests, instead of being reported to the police or defrocked (removed from the priesthood), were moved to another parish where no one knew their history.

In 2002 the *Boston Globe* Spotlight team, the newspaper's investigative reporting unit, reported on the trials of clergy in the Boston area accused of sexual abuse and the cover-up of these crimes by Cardinal Bernard Francis Law. The scandal turned into a major crisis for the Church, not only in the United States, but around the world. The media publicized similar abuses and cover-ups in Ireland, the Philippines, Germany, and in fact everywhere there were Catholics.

Although the priests who had committed these crimes

were a small percentage of all Catholic priests, the public held the Church responsible. The general view was that the Church needed to admit the facts, express remorse, and do everything possible to heal the victims and prevent future abuses. But there was a roadblock to coping with this crisis: some people at the highest levels were shielding the abusers.

Pope John Paul II, although old and ill, was still a powerful spiritual leader of the Church. But he was not able to govern the Curia, the collection of departments that conduct the business of the global Church. One man of great power in the Curia was John Paul II's secretary of state, Cardinal Angelo Sodano. Sodano had financial ties to Father Marcial Maciel, the leader of the ultraconservative order of the Legionaries of Christ in Mexico, and he ignored reports that Maciel was a pedophile. He encouraged the pope to drop the investigation of Maciel.

At the same time that the Church was struggling with the clergy abuse crisis, Argentina suffered another economic meltdown. The peso lost almost half its value. The government, while still paying huge interest on the enormous foreign debt, stopped paying its employees. Then, running out of money completely, it defaulted—gave up paying even the interest on the foreign debt. With the country's banks about to fail, people mobbed the banks to withdraw their money. Millions of people lost their life savings.

More and more Argentinians were thrown out of work, until unemployment reached 40 percent. Middle-class families suddenly found themselves poor. In the early 1970s, less than a tenth of the population had lived below the poverty line, but now more than half were poverty-stricken.

The unions held several strikes to protest layoffs and reduced wages. In some places starving people rioted and looted supermarkets, and Fernando de la Rúa, who had been elected president in 1999, declared a state of emergency. Citizens were so enraged that they filled the Plaza de Mayo in huge demonstrations in front of the Casa Rosada. Banging pots and pans, they demanded that de la Rúa's government resign.

Cardinal Bergoglio did not excuse rioting and looting, but his sympathy was with the unemployed workers. "They don't feel like they really exist," he told interviewers some years later. "No matter how much help they might have from their family or friends, they want to work."

From his office window, Bergoglio saw the police attacking peaceful protesters down in the Plaza de Mayo. He called the Ministry of the Interior to demand a stop to the violence. But many people were wounded, and a few were even killed in the square. On December 20, 2001, President de la Rúa resigned, climbed into his helicopter, and departed hastily from the roof of the Casa Rosada.

Even though de la Rúa was gone, the economic crisis continued for the next two years. Argentinians coined a new word, *cartonero*, for a new occupation: desperate unemployed workers combed trash piles for recyclable material, such as pieces of cardboard, which could be sold to recyclers for a little money. Whereas in the past, Europeans had emigrated from Europe to Argentina for a better life, now thousands of their descendants left Argentina and moved back to Europe for a better life.

In the midst of all this misery and chaos, the Church in Buenos Aires provided a safety net. Bergoglio organized the priests, nuns, monks, and laypeople of each Catholic parish to go out and bring hungry people into the soup kitchens. The churches offered a safe place to sleep for the homeless, and they built shelters.

As the interim president, Eduardo Duhalde, took

office, Cardinal Bergoglio wrote him an open letter that bluntly summarized the shameful record of Argentine governments. Through the years, whether the government was capitalist or socialist, Peronist or military, it had always failed to serve the people of Argentina. "We bishops are sick of systems that produce poor people for the Church to look after," he declared. "Just forty percent of state assistance reaches those who need it, while the rest vanishes along the way because of corruption."

Bergoglio hoped to build a way for Argentinians to work together, after so many years of political strife. With the cooperation of President Duhalde and the help of the United Nations, he and other bishops organized the Diálogo Argentino, a cooperation among groups providing emergency relief. Thousands of civic organizations and many religious communities of various faiths joined efforts to provide food, housing, and health care. They also discussed the problems plaguing Argentine society and agreed on some common solutions.

Then in 2003 Néstor Kirchner, governor of the state of Santa Cruz, in southern Argentina, won the election for president. But he was not supported by the majority of voters. His way of building his political power was confrontation, rather than the cooperation Bergoglio was trying to promote. Kirchner claimed to be for the people, and against the corrupt upper classes and the Church. The enemies of the people, he said, were the generals, the bankers, the exporters—and the bishops.

In Argentina, May 25 is a national holiday, celebrating the country's independence from Spain in 1810. Because of the close connection between the Catholic Church and the government, the day was traditionally observed with a service of thanksgiving, or *Te Deum* Mass, in the cathedral of Buenos Aires. The archbishop of Buenos Aires presided and preached the homily, and important government officials, especially the president, attended. On these occasions, no one expected any critical words from the pulpit.

But as soon as Jorge Bergoglio became archbishop, he began using the *Te Deum* to express his frank opinions about the government. In 1998, with President Carlos Menem in the pews, Bergoglio had pointed out the divide between the few wealthy people and the many impoverished people in Argentina. The next president, de la Rúa, had to listen to Archbishop Bergoglio stating that his government had brought Argentina "into a period of dark shadow."

At the *Te Deum* Mass in 2004, Cardinal Bergoglio preached against intolerance and hatred. "Copying the hate and violence of the tyrant and the murderer is the best way to inherit it." He explained later that he included the Church itself, as well as Kirchner's government, in this warning. But President Kirchner was still offended.

Whether the government cooperated or not, Bergoglio continued to do all he could to promote cooperation among Argentinians. As archbishop of Buenos Aires, he demonstrated that the Catholic Church was open to dialogue with other Christians. He outraged conservative Catholics by meeting with the Protestant evangelicals, the very denominations that were "stealing" converts from the Catholic Church in Latin America.

Churches Compete for Members in Lain America

For centuries after the Spaniards landed in Latin America, almost all the Christians in that region were Catholic. During most of the twentieth century, about 90 percent were Catholic. But by 2014, only 69 percent considered themselves Catholic. On the other hand, 19 percent of Latin Americans identified as Protestants.

The main growth in Protestants in Latin American

countries was in evangelical churches. Many Catholics converting to these Protestant churches explained that they were looking for a more personal relationship with God. Also, they enjoyed the lively style of worship of the evangelical churches. (Some Latin American priests referred scornfully to the Protestant Evangelical movement as an *escuela de samba*, a popular kind of parade with loud samba music, singing, and dancing.)

In June 2006, speaking to a stadium full of Protestants as well as Catholics, Cardinal Bergoglio called aloud on God to unite Christian churches. Then he knelt down on the stage and asked everyone in the stadium to pray for him. The amazing picture of the most powerful religious figure in Argentina kneeling, with Protestant pastors praying over him, appeared in the newspaper *La Nacion*. Ten years afterward, some Catholics were still calling him a "traitor to the faith" for that gesture.

Bergoglio also reached out to other faiths, to Muslims and Jews. He visited mosques and synagogues; he became good friends with a leader of the Jewish community, Rabbi Abraham Skorka. Bergoglio and Skorka eventually wrote a book together, *On Heaven and Earth* (published in 2010), a collection of their long conversations.

Meanwhile, President Kirchner worked to divide Argentine society into "us" against "them." He was a former sympathizer with the Montoneros, the leftist rebels who had fought against the military dictatorship in the 1970s. Immediately after Kirchner's election to the presidency in 2003, he repealed the amnesty, or general pardon, laws passed in 1989 under President Alfosín. Kirchner reopened investigations into the crimes committed by the dictatorship when it ruled Argentina.

Videla, the first president of the military dictatorship, had been tried and convicted in 1985, along with a few others. They had served a few years of their prison terms before the next president, Menem, declared amnesty and freed the prisoners. But there were many who had never been punished at all for their crimes during that era. In 1998 General Videla had been tried and convicted for involvement in the kidnappings, but after a few weeks he was moved to house arrest on the grounds of bad health.

There was a problem with President Kirchner's move in 2003 to investigate and punish crimes committed during the Dirty War: he completely ignored the bombings, kidnappings, and assassinations committed by the Montoneros and other leftist rebels. Many innocent people had suffered from leftist violence, but their victims were not compensated.

In February 2005 the journalist Horacio Verbitsky published a book titled *El Silencio* (*The Silence*). Its subtitle was, *From Paul VI to Bergoglio: The Secret Links Between the Church and the Navy Mechanics School.* The Navy Mechanics School in Buenos Aires, known as ESMA, had been a major detention and torture center for the dictatorship.

Verbitsky was a former Montonero and a political ally of President Kirchner and his wife, Cristina Kirchner. In his book he repeated the accusation from 1986 by Emilio Mignone, father of the kidnapped and "disappeared" Mónica, against Jorge Bergoglio. Verbitsky claimed he had new evidence that the archbishop, as Jesuit provincial in 1977, had betrayed his priests Orlando Yorio and Franz Jalics to the dictatorship. However, the new "evidence" turned out to be questionable, and from an unreliable source.

Bergoglio did not respond. Several years later he explained to interviewers, "If I said nothing at the time, it was so as not to dance to anyone's tune, not because I had anything to hide." Also, he felt that the truth would come out in the course of time.

CHAPTER 14

POPEWORTHY?

ON APRIL 2, 2005, AFTER MANY YEARS OF DECLINING health, Pope John Paul II died. Kings and queens, presidents and prime ministers from around the world flew to Rome for his funeral. Cardinal Bergoglio came too, along with the other cardinals from all nations. Since Pope John Paul II had been pope for such a long time—twenty-seven years—the great majority of the cardinals had never taken part in such a meeting. Many of them did not know one another, and yet they would have to choose the new pope.

The Papacy

According to Roman Catholic doctrine, all the popes, from the first century to the twenty-first, have been successors to Jesus's disciple Peter. In the Gospel of Matthew, Jesus calls Peter (originally named Simon) the "rock" on which he will build his church. However, Peter and his early successors were known as "the bishop of Rome." There was no central authority in the Church to settle questions of doctrine.

In the fourth century, Emperor Constantine (306–337 CE) made Christianity the official religion of the Roman Empire. The bishop of Rome, the capital of the Empire, naturally gained prestige, and most of the bishops in Europe accepted his leadership. The term "pope" was first used in the fourth century to refer to the bishop of Rome Damasus I.

Over the centuries, the pope's authority, based on his direct line of succession from Saint Peter, increased in the Western Church. However, the Eastern Churches never agreed that the pope was supreme. In 1054 the two branches of the Church split.

Meanwhile, the papacy gained political power as well as spiritual authority, acquiring a group of territories, the Papal States. They collected taxes, waged war, and signed treaties just as secular states did. In the medieval and Renaissance periods, the pope often had as much political clout and wealth as any secular ruler. The Protestant Reformation of the sixteenth century accused the popes of having become worldly kings and emperors, and therefore they rejected the pope's leadership.

A REAL-LIFE STORY

In 1871, the Papal States were finally absorbed by the new kingdom of Italy. About the same time, the First Vatican Council (1869–1870) adopted the doctrine of papal infallibility. According to this doctrine, when the pope speaks to define a matter of morals or faith for the entire Catholic Church, his teaching partakes of Christ's divine authority. Under these circumstances, he cannot be mistaken.

After nine days of mourning, ending with the funeral, the cardinals spent a week in general meetings. In the evenings there were private dinners to promote one candidate or another to be the next pope. By custom, no one was supposed to strive for the position. In fact, if a candidate did seem eager to become pope, he would certainly not be elected.

However, different groups of cardinals could agree on the candidate to back and quietly lobby for that man. Among the cardinals eligible for the office in 2005, the favorite was Joseph Ratzinger. He held the important Vatican office of prefect of the Congregation for the Doctrine of the Faith. Ratzinger, a German, was a highly respected theologian. He had years of experience in the Curia, the administration of the worldwide Church.

On the other hand, there had been talk in recent years that the next pope would be Latin American. One of the names mentioned was Cláudio Hummes, archbishop of São Paulo, Brazil. Jorge Bergoglio was not widely known outside of Argentina, and he did not take part in the politicking. He turned down invitations to the private dinners. Outside of the daily meetings, he did not spend time with the other cardinals.

In spite of that, there were evidently some who feared Cardinal Bergoglio could be considered *papabile*, or "popeworthy," when the voting started. A few days before the conclave, the actual election process, a human rights lawyer in Buenos Aires brought a lawsuit against Bergoglio. Using the accusations in Verbitsky's book, he charged that back in 1977 Bergoglio had helped the dictatorship kidnap Orlando Yorio and Franz Jalics.

At the same time, many of the cardinals in Rome received an anonymous message summarizing these accusations from the time of the Dirty War. The sender could have been an ally of President Néstor Kirchner. Or one of the anti-Bergoglio Jesuits, or a faction in the Vatican.

Vatican City

A 110-acre walled city-state within the city of Rome, Vatican City is an independent political body (the smallest in the world) with its own postal system, courts, and police department. The sovereign authority over Vatican City is the Holy See, the pope's territory as the bishop of Rome. It was formally recognized in 1929 by a treaty with Mussolini's Italy.

However, the site of the Vatican has been a destination for pilgrims since the beginnings of the Church. Saint Peter, traditionally considered the first pope, was martyred there by the Emperor Nero. Construction was begun on the first St. Peter's Basilica by the emperor Constantine in 324. In the ninth century, Pope Leo IV had a wall built around the Vatican to protect the basilica from pirates. And the Vatican has been the pope's principal residence since 1377.

From the eighth century until the nineteenth century, the pope was the political ruler of a good portion of the Italian peninsula, known as the Papal States. The papacy maintained its own armies to protect these territories. Now the only remnant of the papal military is the Swiss Guard, which protects the pope. Established in 1506 by Pope Julius II, the Swiss Guard still wears the blue, red, orange, and yellow Renaissance-style dress uniforms.

Within its small territory, Vatican City holds a trove of cultural treasures that attract millions of tourists every year. The Vatican art museums and the Vatican Library are world-famous; so are the Sistine Chapel, with Michelangelo's famous paintings, and the present St. Peter's Basilica (the largest in the world), finished in 1626.

In any case, the message was clearly sent to prevent Jorge Bergoglio from being elected pope. But the cardinals did not pay it much attention. An American cardinal, Francis George of Chicago, said later, "We all knew about the allegations, and we knew they weren't true."

Meanwhile, Bergoglio followed his usual routine for visits to Rome. He stayed in the same unpretentious guesthouse, the Domus Internationalis Paulus VI, eating meals at the common table. He walked through the cobblestone streets and across the Tiber River to meetings in an assembly hall next to St. Peter's Basilica. In his spare time, he liked to visit the Church of St. Louis of the French and gaze at a painting, *The Calling of Saint Matthew*, by Michelangelo Caravaggio.

The painting shows Matthew counting the money he's extorted from poor people, looking the opposite of saintly. Seeing Jesus pointing at him, choosing him for a disciple, Matthew seems to ask, *Who, me?*

As Bergoglio explained to an interviewer later, "I feel like him. Like Matthew." He felt unworthy but chosen, wanting to hold on to his sins but overcome by Jesus's mercy. Bergoglio expressed the power of that merciful love by making up a Spanish word, *misericordiando*, or "mercy-ing." He felt "mercied" by God.

After the days of discussions, the 115 cardinals moved from their lodgings into the Casa Santa Marta, the Vatican guesthouse. They would live there until after the election. The following afternoon, they processed into the Sistine Chapel for the conclave, the election procedure. "Conclave" means literally "with a key," and a large key would actually lock the door behind them for these meetings.

Secrecy during the conclave is a serious tradition in the process to choose a new pope. When the cardinals enter the Sistine Chapel, they swear an oath not to reveal the details of the election. In spite of this, one cardinal did keep a diary during the 2005 conclave and revealed its contents anonymously afterward.

The setting was dramatically fitting for the election of the leader of the Roman Catholic Church. On the chapel wall loomed Michelangelo Buonarroti's famous painting of the *Last Judgment*, in which Christ judges each human soul to be worthy of either heaven or hell.

In the first round of voting, Bergoglio received ten votes. Ratzinger received forty-seven votes, far more than anyone else, but not the two-thirds majority (seventy-seven) required to win.

The following morning, Ratzinger received sixty-five

votes, and Bergoglio thirty-five. On the next round of voting, it was Ratzinger seventy-two, Bergoglio forty.

By the time the conclave broke for lunch at the Casa Santa Marta, Jorge Bergoglio was very disturbed. Going around to the fellow cardinals who had probably voted for him, he urged them to cast their next votes for Ratzinger. The worst thing that could happen, in his view, was for the conclave to divide into opposing parties. Besides, Bergoglio liked and admired Ratzinger, and he thought he should be pope.

That afternoon, April 19, 2005, Joseph Ratzinger received eighty-four votes. He was the new pope, Benedict XVI.

Bergoglio returned happily to Buenos Aires. It was his home, where his friends and loved ones lived, and the time he spent with them was precious. He regularly visited Sister Dolores, the nun who had taught him the catechism, at the Sisters of Mercy Convent. By 2006 she was paralyzed, but her mind was still clear, and she still had a lively sense of fun.

As Bergoglio carried her to her room, he would challenge her to tell the other nuns what he was like as a little boy.

"You were terrible, terrible, as naughty as anything!" she would answer, sending the sisters into fits of laughter. When she died in 2006, Bergoglio prayed all night next to her body in the convent chapel.

During Néstor Kirchner's first term as president of Argentina, the economy recovery that President Duhalde had set in motion continued. Kirchner renegotiated and paid off Argentina's enormous foreign debt. He returned to government control the important industries that Menem had privatized, and he invested in public works and public services.

Kirchner felt he deserved credit for these achievements, and he was angry when Cardinal Bergoglio criticized him as freely as he had other politicians. But Bergoglio knew that the slum-dwellers' lives had not improved much. Twenty-five percent of the population still lived in poverty.

On May 25, 2006, during the traditional *Te Deum* celebration of Argentina's national independence, Bergoglio preached on the Beatitudes, Jesus's sermon about true blessings. The cardinal added a few beatitudes of his own, including, "Blessed are we when we stand against hatred and permanent confrontation, because we do not want the

chaos and disorder which leave us hostages to empires."
Kirchner, listening from his seat of honor in the cathedral,
knew that was aimed at him, and he was furious. He never
entered the cathedral again.

Later that year, during a pilgrimage to the shrine of
Our Lady of Luján, Bergoglio criticized the elites who
encouraged divisions among the people. He prayed for
the people of Argentina to live in harmony. The media
reported Bergoglio's remarks as criticisms of Kirchner's
government—which they were, although Bergoglio
would not confirm that. Kirchner was only further convinced that Bergoglio was his political enemy, and he was
determined to treat him as such. The government's intelligence agency began eavesdropping on Bergoglio's office
from an unmarked white truck parked outside the Church
offices on the Plaza de Mayo.

The way Bergoglio found out about the eavesdropping
was that the driver of the truck came to him and con-
fessed. Bergoglio didn't want the driver to lose his job, so
he didn't complain to the government. Instead he played
classical music in his office, very loud, to keep the truck's
aerials from picking up his conversations.

• • •

While Bergoglio avoided giving interviews and tried to keep himself in the background, he was gradually becoming known in the Catholic Church throughout Latin America. Bergoglio passionately believed that Latin America had a leadership role to play in the future of the worldwide Church. Toward the end of 2005, he was elected president of the Argentine bishops. In May 2007 he attended the fifth conference of the Latin American bishops' confederation (CELAM) in Aparecida, Brazil.

The setting for the conference was carefully chosen. Our Lady of Aparecida, considered the patroness of Brazil, was a small, blackened wooden statue of Mary, the Mother of Jesus. The statue had been discovered by fishermen in their nets in 1717. The shrine of the Black Madonna was a holy place of pilgrimage for millions of believers every year, and many miracles were attributed to her. So the CELAM conference took place at a major focus of popular piety.

Pope John Paul II had run the Church from Rome with a strong hand, discouraging the regions within the Church, such as Latin America, from developing their distinctive voices. But Pope Benedict XVI was sympathetic to allowing the regions more independence. He was especially hopeful that Latin America would renew the Church. In an opening speech, the pope gave his blessing to the three-week Aparecida conference.

During the meetings, Cardinal Bergoglio gave a homily that actually drew applause from the congregation. He spoke forcefully of the plight of the poor in Latin America. While the economies of the Latin American countries had improved in recent years, he pointed out, they had not reduced the misery of the poor.

Bergoglio was elected to write the concluding document of the conference. He gathered the thoughts of numerous different committees from all the member countries. The bishops at the conference were amazed at Cardinal Bergoglio's political skill. His thin figure seemed to be everywhere, consulting with all the different groups. Somehow he stayed calm and cheerful and kept himself in the background. Working this way, he forged the various thoughts into a statement that was acceptable to everyone.

Furthermore, the finished statement was eloquent. It affirmed the "preferential option for the poor" expressed by the first CELAM conference in 1968, in Medellín. It declared that social structures that kept people poor were not only regrettable; they were sinful.

Calling for the renewal of Catholic faith through popular piety, the statement urged priests and bishops to practice a missionary religion. The Church should not wait in cathedrals for people to come to them, but go out into the streets and meet people where they actually lived. By living the Gospel in the slums, they could bring that faith back to the central Church.

While Jorge Bergoglio was becoming known throughout Latin America, he never lost sight of the individual people whom he was called to serve. Bergoglio rarely gave interviews, but he did tell a Catholic journalist the story of a poor widow with seven unbaptized children. He had happened to meet her at the celebration of Saint Cajetan's feast day. Saint Cajetan, or San Cayetano in Spanish, was the patron saint of bread and work. Bergoglio had begun leading huge processions to his shrine on the western edge of the city in 1997, to highlight the crisis of unemployment.

This widow explained to Archbishop Bergoglio (known in the *villas* as "Padre Jorge") that she wanted to have her children baptized. She was very worried about it. But she didn't have the money to pay for a proper baptism party, or to bring the godparents to Buenos Aires.

Bergoglio discussed the problems with her several times, and finally he invited the whole family to his chapel for the baptisms. He performed the ceremony himself, and he provided Coke and sandwiches for the party.

"Father, I can't believe it," the mother told him. "You make me feel important."

"But *Señora*, where do I come in?" he answered. "Jesus is the one who makes you important."

Bergoglio angered some conservative Catholics by breaking what they considered the "rules" of the Church. Many Catholics felt that the children of unmarried parents should not be baptized, and some priests refused to baptize such children. "The child has no responsibility for the marital state of his parents," Bergoglio reminded them. Furthermore, a child's baptism could make a connection whereby the priest could lead the parents into marriage and a lasting relationship with the Church.

One priest in Buenos Aires who was clearly carrying out Bergoglio's vision for the Church was Father José María di Paola, known as Padre Pepe. He was the priest who, in 1997, had brought the statue of the Virgin of Caacupé to Villa 21. He was doing the kind of work that Jorge Bergoglio had done in the poor neighborhoods of San Miguel years ago: building schools and opening soup kitchens, day care centers, housing for the elderly, and chapels. He had become the leader of the slum priests of Buenos Aires.

It was Padre Pepe who launched a campaign against *paco*, a kind of crack cocaine. *Paco* was cheap and very addictive, and it destroyed many lives—and it was also very profitable for drug dealers. Padre Pepe set up a recovery center for addicts and launched a project to educate young people about drugs. The campaign was successful, and Cardinal Bergoglio posted pictures of some of the recovered addicts on the walls of his room.

The antidrug campaign was *so* successful that in 2009 the drug lords sent Padre Pepe a death threat. Padre Pepe, frightened, told the cardinal. Bergoglio immediately went to Villas 21 and 24 himself. He walked around the entire slum in an unhurried way, chatting with people, sharing maté, and blessing them. It was a deliberate signal to the drug lords: "Padre Pepe is under my protection. If you dare to kill someone, kill me."

Bergoglio followed up this visit with an outdoor Mass in the Plaza de Mayo, covered by television crews. In his homily he denounced the drug dealers, calling them "merchants of darkness." And he promoted Padre Pepe to a new position, Vicar of All Slums.

Meanwhile, the Bergoglio family of Jorge's youth was dwindling. His sister Marta had died in 2007. In June 2010 Bergoglio's brother Alberto died. His friend Rabbi Abraham Skorka went with him to the wake. That year, the Catholic priest and the Jewish rabbi were meeting regularly to discuss spiritual questions. Bergoglio had already written a prologue to a book of Skorka's. And Skorka had written a prologue to *El Jesuita* (*The Jesuit*), a series of interviews with Jorge Bergoglio by the journalists Sergio Rubin and Francesca Ambrogetti.

At the wake for Alberto, Skorka asked Bergoglio, for the first time, why he had asked him, a Jew, to write the prologue to such a personal book. Bergoglio answered simply, "It came out of my heart."

On the political scene, President Kirchner had marked the Catholic Church, represented by Cardinal Bergoglio, as his enemy. The middle class in Argentina had prospered during the presidency of Néstor Kirchner, and also after Cristina Kirchner's election as president in 2007. But Bergoglio kept pointing out that unemployment was still high. The poor still lived in slums, and in fact their numbers had grown. *Los descartables*, "throwaway people," Bergoglio called them. Thousands of children in the *villas miserias* still went hungry.

The Kirchners were determined to break Bergoglio's power in Argentina. Néstor Kirchner himself died in October 2010, but his wife, Cristina Kirchner, had been elected president in 2007, and she shared her husband's political goals. They had a fierce ally in the journalist, and former Montonero, Horacio Verbitsky. His book *El Silencio* had been the basis for the lawsuit against Bergoglio, as well as the malicious rumors spread before the papal election, in 2005. As the government conducted a lengthy reinvestigation of crimes committed during the last dictatorship, Verbitsky made sure the accusations against Bergoglio did not go away.

In November 2010, Cardinal Bergoglio was required to give legal testimony as to what he knew about the disappearances, especially the kidnapping of Yorio and Jalics. Bergoglio's press officer, Federico Wals, wanted to contact some of the people Bergoglio had helped escape from the dictatorship, and have them tell their stories. But Bergoglio asked him not to.

Bergoglio was called as a witness, not as an accused

person on trial, and he was allowed to testify in his offices in Buenos Aires, rather than in a courthouse. However, the prosecuting attorney, Luis Zamora, questioned him with the clear purpose of turning up evidence to convict him. Bergoglio gave four hours of testimony, calmly stating the facts. The three judges ruled that the cardinal had no legal responsibility for the kidnappings. But they did convict Admiral Oscar Montes, former foreign minister under President Videla, as well as several others.

Bergoglio was called to the witness stand again in 2011 to answer charges brought against him by some of the Grandmothers of the Plaza de Mayo. They accused him of knowing, during the military dictatorship, that the Church was helping to take babies from the prisoners and put them in "good Catholic homes."

The Grandmothers of the Plaza de Mayo

Of all the crimes committed by the military dictatorship against the citizens of Argentina, perhaps the cruelest was their treatment of the Grandmothers of the Plaza de Mayo. The Grandmothers were women whose daughters had been pregnant at the time they were kidnapped. The young women had been held in secret prisons until they gave birth, and then they were murdered. Their babies were given to other families, often military families, to adopt. It was estimated that about five hundred children had been stolen in this way, or kidnapped from their families as very young children.

By 1998, fifty-six of the kidnapped children had been found, and thirty-one of them reunited with their relatives. In some other cases, the adoptive and the biological families agreed to raise the children jointly. Still other cases turned into court custody battles over the children. But most of the Grandmothers only hoped to find their grandchildren. They marched in the Plaza de Mayo, pleaded with government and Church officials for information, and told their heart-wrenching stories to the media as they had all these years.

Since the dictatorship ended in 1983, by the late 1990s many of the kidnapped children had become adults. The Grandmothers therefore began a public awareness campaign targeted at young people who suspected they might have been kidnapped and adopted. These people could contact the Grandmothers of the Plaza de Mayo to have their blood sampled and the DNA checked. The president of the Grandmothers, Estela de Carlotto, was finally united with her grandson in 2014 when he came forward for a DNA test.

Bergoglio stated that he had not known, and he said nothing against the Grandmothers, even though some of them had attacked him harshly. As he had explained earlier in *El Jesuita*, "We have to put ourselves in the place of a mother whose children were kidnapped and who never heard any more about them."

By this time Bergoglio felt that his assignment as archbishop of Buenos Aires must be nearing the end. He knew that some in the Vatican were planning to remove him from Buenos Aires by assigning him to head a Vatican department in Rome. They could then appoint a more conservative archbishop.

There was nothing Bergoglio could do to prevent being replaced as archbishop, and he feared that all his work to reform the archdiocese might be undone. But in any case, he was determined not to leave his beloved home, Buenos Aires. "They'll never drag me to Rome," he told Federico Wals. Bergoglio intended to retire instead. He had already chosen his room in the clergy retirement home in Flores, the section of Buenos Aires where he had grown up.

In December 2011 Bergoglio turned seventy-five, and he submitted his resignation to the pope. This letter of resignation was a matter of form; bishops were required to resign at the age of seventy-five, and the resignation might or might not be accepted. For the time being, Pope Benedict did not accept Bergoglio's resignation.

CHAPTER 15

"I CHOOSE THE NAME FRANCIS"

AT CELAM 2007, THE LATIN AMERICAN BISHOPS' meeting in Aparecida, Cardinal Bergoglio had summed up a vision of a Church that went outside itself to find people. The Church needed to go to the "peripheries," the margins. It was not just that the people in the *villas miserias* were more receptive to the Good News than the people in the comfortable neighborhoods. It was also that the Church could learn from poor and oppressed people to renew its own faith.

And the Church in Europe, Bergoglio believed, had

much to learn from Latin America. The vigor of the Latin American Church showed in the CELAM meeting itself, in the enthusiastic way the bishops from all over the continent worked together. Pope Benedict himself hoped that Latin America would be the source to inspire the world Church.

From Pope Zachary of Greece in the eighth century through Benedict XVI, a German, in the twenty-first century, the pope had always been a European. This made some sense during the years that most members of the Roman Catholic Church lived in Europe.

However, the balance shifted during the twentieth century. By 2012, most Catholics did *not* live in Europe, and this had been true for many years. Over 40 percent of the world's Catholics lived in Latin America, and the fastest-growing Catholic group was in Africa.

The problem was not only that most of the world's Catholics were non-European. The biggest problem was that the European Church was old, tired, and focused on defending itself. As Cardinal Carlo Maria Martini, former archbishop of Milan, said shortly before his death in 2012, "The Church is tired, in the Europe of well-being, and in America. Our culture has aged, our churches are big and empty and the church bureaucracy rises up, and our rites and vestments are pompous."

As Bergoglio had told the interviewers for *El Jesuita* (later republished as *Pope Francis: Conversations with Jorge Bergoglio; His Life in His Own Words*), a Church closed in on itself "will deteriorate like the inside of a locked room, mold and damp spreading everywhere." A church "that only watches over its small flock is a church that, in the long term, becomes sick." He added one of his original turns of phrase: "The shepherd who locks himself in is not a true pastor for his sheep, but just a 'hairdresser' for sheep, putting in their curlers."

Bergoglio's fresh, inventive way with words caught his listeners' attention. They called his original expressions, such as his new verb "mercied," "bergoglisms." Some admirers began to collect them. In a retreat he led in 2012, Bergoglio criticized a Church that thought it was self-sufficient, that "had Jesus tied up in the sacristy" and wouldn't let him out.

While Jorge Bergoglio was full of energy and eager to share his vision with others, Pope Benedict XVI was thinking about leaving office. He had not been young when he was elected in 2005, at the age of seventy-eight. In fact, *before* his election, he had already tried to retire three times. But Pope John Paul II had refused his resignations.

Benedict had struggled to reform the Curia, including some of the suspicious practices at the Vatican Bank. Faced with the ongoing scandal of sexual abuse by priests and cover-ups, he had denounced Marcial Maciel, the founder of a Mexican order, the Legionaries of Christ, and brought proceedings against him.

Early in 2012, after a bad fall, Benedict concluded that he no longer had the health or strength to carry out his duties as leader of the world's 1.2 billion Roman Catholics. His hearing was bad, and he had lost the sight in one eye. He was thin and exhausted. In April, he turned eighty-five.

Before Benedict could announce his decision to retire, a fresh scandal, known as "Vatileaks," broke out. In May 2012 the media published documents from the pope's desk, given to them by the pope's butler, revealing the shocking extent of corruption and money laundering. It looked to the world as if Benedict XVI was helpless to control his administration.

On February 11, 2013, Benedict announced that he would resign on February 28. The world was shocked. The last time a pope had resigned, rather than serving until his death, was 1415. But Cardinal Bergoglio praised the pope's decision as "courageous and revolutionary."

Once again, the cardinals of the Roman Catholic Church were called together in Rome to elect a new pope. The Vatican sent Bergoglio a first-class plane ticket, but in his usual style, he exchanged it for a coach seat. The priests who worked at the Buenos Aires cathedral thought he ought to have new shoes, since his old ones were shabby from walking the streets of the *villas miserias*. They gave him a new pair for the trip.

Before leaving Buenos Aires, Jorge Bergoglio called his sister María Elena. By this time, they were the only two left of the five Bergoglio brothers and sisters, and he called her every week for a long chat. "Have a nice trip," she told him. "I'll see you when you get back." The next day, February 26, the cardinal took off for Rome—wearing his old shoes.

Meanwhile, all over the world the Vatican watchers speculated in the newspapers, on the radio, and on TV as to who the next pope would be. They thought he would probably be the Italian archbishop of Milan, Cardinal Angelo Scola, or maybe the Canadian Marc Ouellet. One of the longer shots was Cardinal Sean O'Malley, arch-bishop of Boston.

The speculators agreed that if the conclave chose a Latin American, he would most likely be Odilo Scherer of Brazil. (María Elena herself hoped Scherer would be elected, because she felt he was on the side of the poor.) Another Latin American mentioned was Leonardo Sandri, Bergoglio's fellow seminary student from long ago. Cardinal Jorge Bergoglio of Argentina had managed to keep such a low profile, by refusing interviews and staying in the back-ground, that almost none of the Vatican watchers thought of him. Besides, he was seventy-six. Perhaps that was why before this conclave no one tried to recirculate the accusa-tions against him from the Dirty War.

In Rome, Bergoglio checked into room 203 in the Domus Internationalis Paulus VI, the guesthouse where he always stayed on these trips. Every morning, he put on his worn black shoes and walked through the streets of the city to the pre-conclave meetings of the cardinals. He was bothered with sciatica, a sharp pain, in one leg, but he liked to be out on the streets mingling with ordinary people, just as he did at home. His black raincoat covered the cross around his neck, and he did not wear his telltale red cardinal's skullcap. On his wrist was his black plastic watch.

In the meeting hall the 115 cardinals began to discuss the state of the world Church. They generally agreed that the new pope should be a strong administrator, unlike either Benedict XVI or John Paul II, to control the corruption and dysfunction in the Curia, the central administration governing the worldwide Roman Catholic Church. But he should not be authoritarian, like John Paul II, or detached and ill-informed, like Benedict XVI. He should encourage communication from local branches of the Church and be ready to share authority with them. It was suggested that the pope needed a council of cardinals—ones who were *not* Vatican insiders—to advise him.

As the discussions went on, the cardinals who had voted for Bergoglio in 2005, including Cardinal Murphy-O'Connor of England, began to lobby on his behalf. They argued that Bergoglio's age was not necessarily a drawback— Benedict had just shown that a pope could retire. Bergoglio had proven, at least to the Latin American cardinals, that he was a highly effective leader. And he was a man of authentic humility, living simply and working with the poor.

On the morning of March 7, after several days of

meetings, Bergoglio rose to make a short but forceful speech. "The only purpose of the Church is to go out to tell the world the good news about Jesus Christ," he said in his fluent Italian. "The Church has got too wrapped up in itself. . . . The next pope should be someone who helps the Church surge forth to the peripheries." This was the kind of inspiration the cardinals had been waiting for.

The conclave began the following Tuesday, March 12. It was a cold, rainy day. Bergoglio and the rest of the cardinals moved into the Casa Santa Marta, the Vatican guesthouse, as they had in 2005. Bergoglio's room number was 207. In order to conduct the conclave in absolute secrecy, they had to turn in their cell phones and tablets. This rule bothered some of the cardinals, but not Cardinal Bergoglio. He had never used any device more technologically advanced than a landline telephone.

That morning, the cardinals were bused to St. Peter's Basilica for a special Mass before they went into the conclave. A storm, dramatic with thunder and lightning and even hail, raged outside during the Mass. The ceremony inside, also dramatic, was televised and watched all over the world. One hundred and fifteen cardinals, robed in scarlet, processed to the high altar and kissed it.

After lunch, the 115 elector cardinals returned to St. Peter's. This time, they processed into the Sistine Chapel, singing the ancient Latin hymn "Veni, Creator Spiritus," calling on the Holy Spirit to guide their minds as they decided and voted. They took oaths to keep the proceedings of the conclave secret, to disregard any instructions other than the Church's—and, if elected pope, to "defend the liberty of the Holy See." The door was locked behind them. The conclave was in session.

The cardinals sat in four long rows of tables, two rows on each side of the chapel. One by one, carrying their folded paper ballots, they walked to the altar at the front of the chapel, knelt, and declared in Latin that they were voting for the man they believed should be pope. The ballot was placed in a huge silver chalice. After everyone had voted, the ballots were read out loud and tallied.

In this conclave, unlike 2005, no cardinal kept a secret diary of the exact tallies (or if he did, he didn't share it). But from what various electors said afterward, no one won a majority of votes that afternoon, although Bergoglio won at least twenty-five, a respectable number. Clearly, he was *papabile*—it was possible that he could be elected pope. The cardinals returned to the Casa Santa Marta.

At dinner, Bergoglio sat next to Leonardo Sandri. The two men had known each other since their seminary days, when Bergoglio was the prefect ringing the bell to wake Sandri up in the morning. "Get ready, my friend," Sandri warned Bergoglio.

The next morning, Wednesday, the cardinals went through two more ballots. By the time the conclave broke for lunch, Jorge Mario Bergoglio was ahead, with more than fifty votes of the seventy-seven needed to elect a pope. Cardinal Sean O'Malley of Boston sat next to Bergoglio at lunch and noticed that he hardly ate anything.

The reason for Bergoglio's lack of appetite was not nervousness, though. As he explained later to Antonio Spadaro, editor of the Jesuit magazine *America*, "a deep and inexplicable peace and interior consolation" had come over him. Nothing else, including food, seemed important.

On the first ballot of that afternoon, Bergoglio received nearly, but not quite, seventy-seven votes. There was a technical problem with the second ballot, so those results had to be thrown out. A third round of voting began.

It was almost seven o'clock when the name "*Eminentissimo Bergoglio*" (His Eminence Bergoglio) was read out for the seventy-seventh time. The cardinals in the Sistine

Chapel let out a sigh, as if they had all been holding their breath. They stood and clapped. Probably some of them would have preferred another man. But the most important thing was for the cardinals to agree on the choice of the new pope. They were confident that Jorge Bergoglio would be a reformer, and reform was badly needed in the Church.

The vote counting had to go on to the end, but the pope had been elected. Cardinal Cláudio Hummes from Brazil embraced Bergoglio and said, "Don't forget the poor."

According to custom, Bergoglio was asked in Latin if he accepted his election as Supreme Pontiff. "*Accepto*," he replied. He added, also in Latin, "I am a sinner, but I trust in the infinite mercy and patience of our Lord Jesus Christ, and I accept in a spirit of penance."

Again according to custom, Bergoglio was asked what name he would take as pope. "I choose the name Francis, in honor of Saint Francis of Assisi." This was a surprise— there had never been a pope named Francis. But it made perfect sense to Bergoglio, especially after what Cardinal Hummes, a Franciscan, had said. As Bergoglio explained at a press conference later, Francis of Assisi was "the man of poverty, the man of peace."

Bergoglio, now Francis, left the chapel to change from his red cardinal's clothes to the white cassock and skullcap of the pope. He was offered red papal shoes, in five different sizes, but he shook his head. Still wearing his old black shoes, he returned to the Sistine Chapel, to be greeted as pope by each of the remaining cardinals. Then he started toward the balcony where he would be presented to the waiting crowds in St. Peter's Square.

But on the way, "I was seized by a great anxiety," as Francis described it later. He felt the crushing weight of the responsibility he had just accepted. Turning aside into the chapel of St. Paul, he sat down in a back pew and prayed.

Francis's prayer was answered with a sense of "great light." Confident that God was with him, he left the chapel smiling.

Father Jorge was now Pope Francis. He would have to live in Rome, not Buenos Aires. He would not be able to ride the subway wearing a plain black cassock, mingling with people unnoticed.

However, Francis kept his way of life as much as possible. For instance, he continued to place his own telephone calls. One of the first people he called was his sister,

María Elena. She had been home, doing housework, when she heard that a pope had been elected.

"We turned on the TV to find out who the poor guy was who had been elected pope," as she told it. When her brother called her, he was laughing, as if his becoming pope was a good joke on both of them. Maybe he was remembering how he had planned to resist being assigned some job in the Vatican. "They'll never drag me to Rome," he had said. Once again, God had sprung a surprise on him.

To María Elena, her brother was still "Jorge," not "Francis," or "Holy Father," the usual title of the pope. "You looked really good on television, you had a radiant expression," María Elena told him. She added wistfully, perhaps already feeling a new distance between them, "I wish I could give you a hug."

"We are hugging," he answered, "we are together. I have you very close to my heart."

Pope Francis also called the newsstand in the Plaza de Mayo to cancel his newspaper subscription. He called his dentist to cancel an appointment. He called his nephew José Luis Narvaja, the Jesuit priest. He called many friends.

But the very first person Francis had called was the retired pope, Benedict XVI. They exchanged good wishes and asked for each other's prayers. Jorge Bergoglio the Argentinian and Joseph Ratzinger the German had much more in common than most people realized.

True, their style was obviously different. Pope Benedict had favored the fancy regalia for his public appearances: the red shoes, the red papal cape trimmed with ermine, a broad-brimmed red hat for outdoor events. Pope Benedict's early career had been as a scholar and theologian, rather than working in a parish, or training novices like Francis. And Benedict was definitely not a political animal like Francis.

But Benedict and Francis liked each other personally, and they had been on good terms ever since the CELAM conference in 2007. Their understanding about spiritual truth was very similar. Like Francis, Benedict respected popular piety as a true expression of Catholic faith. Benedict had been a friend and admirer of the philosopher Guardini, the subject of Bergoglio's unfinished PhD dissertation.

One of the sacrifices Francis had to make, on becoming pope, was that he could no longer walk around the city or take public transportation. But he was not going to be driven in the papal limousine, either, if he could help it. So the morning after his election, he got into a Vatican police car and asked the driver to make several stops. The pope wanted to pray in some special places, including the chapel where Ignatius of Loyola had celebrated his first Mass. And he wanted to pay his bill at the clergy guesthouse.

The clerk at the desk in the Domus Internationalis stared, dumbfounded, as Francis held out his credit card. "You're the pope," he protested. "You don't have to pay." But Francis insisted. Since he was pope, he said, that was all the more reason he should set a good example. He went on upstairs to pack and, while he was at it, to change a dead lightbulb in his room.

During the next few days, Francis took care of another piece of unfinished business: reconnecting with the Society of Jesus. Although technically Bergoglio was still a Jesuit, he had had almost no contact with them since he left Córdoba in 1992. There was still bad feeling between him and some of the older Jesuits, dating back to Bergoglio's years as provincial, 1973–79.

To begin healing these old wounds, Francis called the Jesuit headquarters in Rome to talk to the superior general of the Society of Jesus, Adolfo Nicolás. "Good morning, it's Pope Francis," he told the receptionist who answered the phone. The young man thought at first that this must be a prankster. When he realized that he really was talking to the pope, he was so embarrassed that Francis had to calm him down.

Francis was finally connected with Nicolás, and they had a cordial conversation and agreed to meet that Sunday, March 17. A few months later, on July 31, 2013, the feast day of Saint Ignatius, Francis celebrated Mass at the Church of the Gesù, the Jesuit mother church in Rome. In his homily to his fellow Jesuits, he spoke of the human failures that all of them had made. After the Mass, he stopped to pray at the tomb of Father Pedro Arrupe, who had inspired and guided him from the time Jorge Bergoglio was a young man.

In spite of the years of estrangement, Bergoglio had never stopped thinking of himself as a Jesuit. Even as a cardinal, he had followed a simple, disciplined way of life. He had always depended on Jesuit spirituality, especially discernment, to guide him. Now that he was pope, he relied as much as ever on discernment "in the presence of the Lord" in making choices, large and small.

• • •

From the beginning of his papacy, Pope Francis did the unexpected. He refused to live in the papal palace, as popes had done for the last century. Instead, he moved into room 201, a modest two-room suite in the Casa Santa Marta. One of the rooms was his bedroom. The room in which he received visitors had a sofa, a few chairs, a small desk, a bookcase, and a crucifix.

Francis brought from Buenos Aires a very few personal things: an icon of Saint Francis, a statue of Our Lady of Luján, and a statue of Saint Joseph. And a chunk of wood from the bleachers of the soccer stadium where he used to watch matches with his father. Jorge Bergoglio had changed his name and his title, but he would not change his loyalty to the San Lorenzo team.

Pope Francis ate in the Casa Santa Marta cafeteria with the workers, and he made them welcome at the daily Mass he celebrated. What bothered him about the thought of living in the palace, he explained, wasn't the luxury, but the isolation. "I need to live my life with others."

Just as when he was made a cardinal, Pope Francis had asked his friends and admirers in Buenos Aires *not* to fly to Rome for his formal inauguration on March 19. Instead, they should give the plane fare money to the poor. He made one important exception, inviting Sergio Sánchez, a leader of the impoverished *cartoneros*, or recycling collectors, of Buenos Aires, to be his guest.

March 19 happened to be the Feast of St. Joseph, the patron saint of Francis's childhood church. The sun shone on a crowd of two hundred thousand gathered for the inauguration. The guests included representatives from 132 nations and international organizations, as well as many religious leaders. For the first time since the Eastern Churches broke with the Roman Catholic Church in 1054, the Orthodox patriarch of Constantinople attended a papal inauguration. Also, for the first time *ever*, the Chief Rabbi of Rome was a guest.

In his homily during the Mass, Francis described what he expected from himself—what he believed God expected of him—in his new role. The pope, he said, "must open his arms to protect all of God's people and embrace with tender affection the whole of humanity, especially the poorest, the weakest, the least important."

After the Mass, Francis rode around St. Peter's Square in an open white SUV, hugging, kissing, and joking with the crowd. Some Latin Americans offered him their gourds of maté, and he took sips. When he spotted a disabled person, he stepped out of the SUV to embrace them. In the future, this would be the style of his weekly audiences in the square.

The night before the inauguration, an enormous crowd had held vigil in Buenos Aires, outside the cathedral in the Plaza de Mayo. It was the kind of joyful fiesta that Jorge Bergoglio loved, with priests hearing confessions as well as rock singers entertaining the crowd. Huge screens around the square stood ready to show the ceremony live from Rome. But the first thing they heard live from Rome, at 3:32 a.m., was Francis's voice—speaking directly to them. He had phoned the cathedral, and they had relayed the call to the loudspeakers in the square.

From across the Atlantic, almost seven thousand miles away, their former archbishop talked lovingly, intimately to his people, using Buenos Aires slang to make them laugh. He asked them to care for each other, and to pray for him. Francis did not say so, but one of the hardest sacrifices he had to make, in becoming pope, was giving up his life with the people of Buenos Aires.

CHAPTER 16

A CHURCH
OF SURPRISES

"GOD IS ALWAYS A SURPRISE," FRANCIS TOLD
Antonio Spadaro, editor of the Jesuit magazine *America*, in
interviews during August 2013. The new pope had already
demonstrated this idea with his own series of surprises.

March 28, 2013, was Holy Thursday, and it was traditional
for the pope to celebrate the evening of the Last Supper in a
cathedral. Instead Francis went to a prison for juvenile offend-
ers. Down on his knees on the stone floor, he washed the feet
of twelve young prisoners. Some of them were Catholic, but
others were Muslim or atheist. Two of them were women.

"Washing your feet means I am at your service," he explained to them. "Help one another: this is what Jesus teaches us." In a lighter touch, at the end of the ceremony he gave each prisoner a chocolate egg and a dove-shaped Easter cake.

This event was a powerful message to the prisoners: *The world may think you're* descartables, *throwaway people, but I do not. In God's eyes, you are cherished.*

It was also a message to anyone in the Church who thought these prisoners were unworthy. Customarily, on Holy Thursday the popes had washed the feet of twelve priests or deacons. And in 1988 John Paul II had issued an edict to all Catholic priests that only *men* should have their feet washed on Holy Thursday. But Francis, as Archbishop Bergoglio, had ignored that rule for years. Now that he was pope, he was all the more determined to show that he meant what he said about embracing the whole of humanity.

Another surprise of Pope Francis's was the destination for his first trip outside Rome. On July 8 he arrived on Lampedusa, a small island in the Mediterranean Sea between Sicily and Libya. Many thousands of refugees, fleeing the civil war in Syria or violence in Sudan and other African countries, had died trying to reach Lampedusa. But more kept coming in overcrowded and rickety crafts. Up until now, the world had paid little attention to this ongoing tragedy.

Francis laid a wreath of flowers on the water where the refugees had drowned. At an altar made of wood from capsized rafts, he said Mass. He prayed for forgiveness for the hard-heartedness of the world, the "culture of comfort" that ignored the desperate migrants. He himself came from a family of immigrants, and it was only good luck that they had not gone down with the *Principessa Mafalda* on their voyage to a new home.

Because Francis was the pope, everything he did was news. So he could use his position to draw attention to the plight of juveniles in prison, and of immigrants fleeing for their lives. Pictures of the Holy Thursday service at the prison and of the Mass on Lampedusa appeared on newspaper front pages, on TV, and all over the Internet.

Francis also used his position to do something he thought the Church should have done years ago: He unblocked the canonization process for Óscar Romero. The archbishop of San Salvador had been killed defending the rights of the poor in 1980, but some in the Vatican had objected to declaring Romero a saint.

Along with these and other dramatic gestures, Francis used the pope's traditional channels. In his first year in office, he published an apostolic exhortation, a sort of open letter to the worldwide Church. It was titled *Evangelii Gaudium*, the Joy of the Gospel.

The pope had blunt words for today's consumer society, satisfied with itself but never satisfied with enough things. He criticized "trickle-down" economic theories that claimed that the free market would bring about "greater justice and inclusiveness." "How can it be that it is not a news item when an elderly homeless person dies of exposure, but it is news when the stock market loses two points?" "God's heart has a special place for the poor, so much so that he himself 'became poor.'" "I want a Church which is poor and for the poor."

Francis's main theme was that spreading the Good News about Jesus Christ was the first and the most important reason for the Church to exist. Furthermore, the only way to draw people to the Christian faith was through joy. "An evangelizer must never look like someone who has just come back from a funeral!"

This statement was a surprise to Mario Poli, the bishop who replaced Bergoglio as archbishop of Buenos Aires.

Visiting the Vatican after Francis's election, he remarked to the new pope that it was a big change to see him smiling all the time. Francis replied, "It's very entertaining to be pope."

It was like Francis to answer with a joke, rather than explain that he hadn't really changed. True, those who met Cardinal Bergoglio in his office or at the cathedral were likely to find him looking serious, even glum. But the people of the *villas miserias* in Buenos Aires who had shared a gourd of maté with Padre Jorge, or celebrated a religious fiesta with him, were not surprised at Pope Francis's joyous smile.

However, it must have been fun for Francis to be in a position where he could "flip the omelet," as he put it. The Church had gotten much too set in its ways, and it needed to be shaken up—surprised. And he clearly enjoyed such moments as posing with a newlywed couple who brought clown therapy to sick children. Bride, groom, and pope were all grinning, wearing red clown noses.

In one of his first sermons, Francis urged priests and bishops to be "shepherds who smelled of sheep." Jesus had called himself "the good shepherd," the one who knew his sheep by name and personally made sure they had food, water, and shelter. Likewise, the leaders in the Church should be sharing the lives of the people—and learning from them as well as teaching them.

Shortly after Pope Francis's appearance on the island of Lampedusa, he traveled to Rio de Janeiro, Brazil, for World Youth Day. To the horror of the security teams guarding him, he refused to ride in a "popemobile," an armored vehicle with bulletproof glass. "A sardine can," he called it. Instead he rode in a small gray Fiat with the windows rolled down.

Francis remembered perfectly well that John Paul II had been shot, almost fatally, in 1981, but he left that danger in God's hands. "I don't want to be in a glass box," he said. "I want to be able to touch, hug, kiss people. Otherwise, what's the point of going to Brazil?"

In Brazil the weather was unusually cold and rainy, but Pope Francis still managed to fit in a side trip to the shrine of the Black Madonna at Aparecida. Almost two hundred thousand pilgrims, shivering under umbrellas, greeted him. Aparecida had been the site of the CELAM (Latin American bishops' conference) in 2007, resulting in a continent-wide declaration for the poor. Francis felt there was a deep connection between that event and his amazing election as pope.

Before leaving Aparecida, Francis moved through the crowd, "touching, hugging, and kissing" just as he intended. Two of the people he joyously embraced were friends from the past, Sergio and Ana Gobulin, whom he had saved from Videla's military dictatorship in Argentina more than thirty years ago. They had been living in Italy ever since, but traveled to Brazil, at the invitation of friends, for the pope's visit.

Back in Rio de Janeiro, Francis stopped at the St. Francis of Assisi Hospital. He met with recovering drug addicts and alcoholics, listening to their stories. He hugged each one and told them, "Do not let yourselves be robbed of hope!"

The pope's schedule was tightly packed, and he was seventy-six, but he seemed inexhaustible. He insisted on fitting in a visit to one of Rio's many shantytowns, called favelas in Brazil. Just as in Buenos Aires, he was invited into a one-room house and spent some time chatting with the family—without cameras or reporters. Then, moving on to the soggy soccer field, he addressed the crowds.

The next two days were planned as gatherings of young people on Copacabana Beach. On the three-mile stretch of sand, he addressed millions of young pilgrims in a way that gave them the feeling that he was speaking personally to each one. His voice was quiet, but his words were electrifying. He urged them to be "athletes of Christ," inviting them to train for a mission more challenging than winning the World Cup: loving and helping others.

On the plane back to Rome, Pope Francis held an in-flight press conference. Pope Benedict's press conferences had been tightly controlled, so the journalists were surprised to hear that they could ask Francis any questions. One of their questions was, Did the pope approve of homosexuality?

Typically, Francis turned the question so that instead of proclaiming a rule about homosexuality in general, he was considering an individual person. "If someone is gay and is searching for the Lord and has good will, then who am I to judge him?" This answer was also a reminder to Christians that their mission was *not* to enforce rules and judge. God would take care of judgment.

However, Francis did not mean to overturn Church doctrine. In the Catholic Church, marriage could be only between a man and a woman. As archbishop of Buenos Aires, Bergoglio had protested a new law in Argentina to allow same-sex marriage, and he had not changed his mind.

The journalists on the plane were also curious about the black briefcase Francis had carried on the plane. In the past, the popes had always let an aide carry their luggage. What was in the briefcase, and why was it so important that he wouldn't let it out of his hands?

"It doesn't contain the key to the atom bomb," Francis joked.

He went on to explain that he always carried his own briefcase—it was only normal. The briefcase contained the things he would need most on a trip: "My razor, my breviary, my diary, [with all his appointments, addresses, and phone numbers], a book to read." The breviary, a book containing the essential Catholic psalms, rites, and prayers, was important in itself—he opened it every morning to pray with the Psalms. But also, tucked into the breviary was the precious letter from Grandma Rosa. He had kept it with him ever since the day of his ordination as a priest.

One of the recommendations of Vatican II, back in the late 1960s, had been that the regional churches should have more responsibility to govern themselves. However,

Pope John Paul II and Benedict XVI had ruled the Church like kings, with authority concentrated in the Vatican. But Francis had believed, for many years before his election, in more independence for the regional and national churches. He also thought that the pope could benefit from the counsel of people throughout the world, outside the Curia.

Now that Francis was the pope, he put these ideas into practice. He appointed a council of eight cardinals (later, nine) to advise him. They were from Africa, India, the United States, and Latin America, as well as Europe, and they were all independent-minded.

Furthermore, Francis took steps to give the international assembly of bishops, the Synod of Bishops, real power, instead of having them rubber-stamp whatever the pope decided. He often referred to himself as "the Bishop of Rome." That was one of the pope's titles, but it downplayed his importance as head of the entire Roman Catholic Church. As his friend and biographer Elisabetta Piqué noted, he hated "being treated like an emperor."

In March 2014 Pope Francis created the Pontifical Commission for the Protection of Minors to deal with the problem of sexual abuse by clergy. He appointed as the head of the commission Cardinal Sean O'Malley of Boston. O'Malley had already done impressive work on sexual abuse crises in the dioceses of Fall River, Massachusetts; Palm Beach, Florida; and Boston. Notably, half of the people appointed to this commission were women.

On a trip to Jerusalem in May 2014, Pope Francis used the occasion to show solidarity with other faiths. He met with Patriarch Bartholomew, the head of the Eastern Orthodox Church. Francis went with Rabbi Abraham Skorka and Imam Omar Abboud to the Western Wall, a remnant of a wall of the ancient Second Temple and a place of pilgrimage. These three friends, Christian, Jewish, and Muslim, prayed together, and then they embraced one another.

Francis liked a saying attributed to Saint Francis of Assisi: "Preach the Gospel always, and if necessary, use words." He knew he could often communicate more with one public act than with thousands of words. So he made his point about peace by visiting a Palestinian refugee camp as well as the Yad Vashem Holocaust memorial. He prayed at the recent concrete wall, twenty-six feet tall, that separated Israel from the Palestinian West Bank.

Although Pope Francis was adored by many Catholics, many other Catholics were unhappy with him. On the conservative-traditional side, some people thought a pope who laughed and joked so much was undignified. They didn't like his suggestions that the Church had overemphasized the sins of abortion and sex outside of marriage, and underemphasized the sin of ignoring poverty.

Conservative Catholics were offended by his implication that they were focused on condemning sins, rather than offering compassion to wounded souls. "I envision the Church as a field hospital after a battle," Francis explained. "The confessional is not a torture chamber but a place of mercy." They didn't like his description of the Church as too closed in on itself, a shut-up room that smells of mold.

Some who denied the danger of climate change felt attacked by Francis's 2015 encyclical on the environment, *Laudato si' (Praise Be): On the Care for Our Common Home.* In this document he criticized consumerism, reckless development, and the pollution of the environment. He called on the people of the world to combat global warming.

On the liberal-progressive side, some were put off by his

insistence that God was a personal presence. "When we talk to God," he explained, "we speak to persons who are concrete and tangible, not some misty, diffuse god-like spray."

Gay activists were disappointed that although he approved of civil unions, he believed that same-sex couples should not adopt children.

Feminists were dismayed at Pope Francis's refusal to reconsider what the Church had maintained for centuries, that women could not be ordained priests. They bristled at the pope's remark (not intended to offend) that the women on his council were like "strawberries on the cake." One woman retorted that if the women were strawberries, the men must be the nuts.

In a proclamation on family life, Francis managed to anger both conservatives and liberals. He urged pastors to be merciful to divorced and remarried Catholics and to welcome them, rather than throwing the rules at them like stones. However, this did not change the Church's position on divorce. Francis also said that homosexual people should be welcome in the Church and never discriminated against—but the Church's position on marriage was that it could only be between a man and a woman.

In September 2015, Pope Francis visited the United States for the first time. He was already popular with almost all American Catholics, as well as many non-Catholics, and huge throngs attended his public appearances in Washington, D.C., New York, and Philadelphia. But again, some of his actions offended conservatives. In his address to a joint session of the U.S. Congress (the first ever for a pope), Francis asked them to end "hostility" toward immigrants. At the United Nations, he denounced the culture of "boundless thirst" for wealth and power.

On the other hand, liberals were dismayed that Francis met privately, at the Vatican Embassy, with Kim Davis. She was the Kentucky county clerk who refused to issue marriage licenses to same-sex couples.

But anyone who labeled Francis as too conservative, or too liberal, was missing the point. In Argentina, presidents with various political views had missed the same point about Cardinal Bergoglio. He was not committed to one ideology or another. He was committed to following Jesus's orders: spread the Good News and support the poor and oppressed.

While he was still a cardinal, Bergoglio had remarked to his press secretary, "I don't understand, the people of the Catholic right see me as on the left, and the people on the left as someone on the right, but I'm a shepherd who wants to walk in the midst of his people."

In spite of the weight of two thousand years of tradition, Francis seemed determined to discern for himself how best to act as the head of the worldwide Roman Catholic Church. He joked to the journalist Jorge Milia, his former student, about the lack of instructions on how to be pope. "I kept looking in Benedict's library, but I couldn't find a user's manual. So I manage as best I can."

Pope Francis continued to surprise (and sometimes offend) with dramatic actions. In February 2016 he ended a trip to Mexico with a celebration of the Mass in Ciudad Juárez, Mexico, just across the southern border of the United States. Francis laid a bouquet of flowers and prayed at a memorial to the thousands of immigrants who lost their lives trying to cross into the United States. Then he waved a blessing to the people watching from El Paso, Texas.

As Francis said Mass for the two hundred thousand people gathered in Juarez, the service was also broadcast live to the Sun Bowl stadium in El Paso. "No border will keep us from sharing," he told the worshippers on both sides of the tall chain-link fence. Since 2016 was an election year in the United States, some politicians criticized his actions as trying to influence U.S. policy toward immigrants.

At the end of July 2016, World Youth Day was held in Krakow, Poland. Before the celebrations began, Pope Francis took a side trip to Auschwitz, the death camp where the Nazis had murdered more than one million people, mostly Jews. He walked alone, limping slightly, under the iron arch with the cynical slogan, *Arbeit Macht Frei* (Work Makes You Free). Inside the gates, he met and kissed several survivors of the camp.

Pope Francis spent a long time in an Auschwitz prison cell where a Polish Franciscan priest, Maximilian Kolbe, had died in the place of a stranger in 1941. Francis simply sat on a chair in the dark cell, his head bent, praying silently. Later he quietly greeted a group of Polish men and women who had risked their lives during the Nazi occupation to help Jews.

Back in Krakow, Francis spoke about how Christians need to stand up to the human rights violations still going on in the world. He pointed out to his listeners that violence, hatred, and terror were not just problems of the past. Terrible suffering, especially among refugees, was going on right now.

At the pope's last Mass in Poland, in a huge field before one million pilgrims, he urged young people to work for social justice. "The times we live in do not call for young couch potatoes, but for young people with . . . boots laced." Many in the audience were inspired. But a Polish official commented that in spite of the pope's words, the government was *not* going to change its policy about immigrants. Like some other Eastern European nations, Poland had decided it would be dangerous to allow Muslim refugees into their country.

Francis didn't know how many years he would continue as pope. "Four or five years; I do not know, even two or three," he told an interviewer in 2015. The pope followed a punishing schedule of work and public events all over the world.

Francis also didn't know how much he could accomplish in whatever time he had. He realized that the next pope could undo many of his reforms. As he told a friend, "The only thing I ask of the Lord is that the changes for which I am making so many personal sacrifices will not be like a light that goes out."

A new pope might dissolve the Council of Cardinal Advisers, giving back power to the Curia. He could discourage the regional bishops' councils from participating in governing the Church. He could encourage Church officials to wear elaborate, costly vestments, ride in luxury limousines, and entertain like royalty. He could put all his effort into enforcing doctrine, the rules of the Church.

But even if Francis's time was short, he was determined not to rush his decisions. "Many think that changes and reforms can take place in a short time. I believe that we always need time to lay the foundations for real, effective change."

In any case, the Catholic Church could never be the same after Francis. Everyone had heard him say, "The name of God is mercy." They had seen him hug a hideously disfigured man, and send blessings across a menacing international border, and welcome families of refugees into the Vatican.

As a high school student, kneeling in his parish church, Jorge Bergoglio had opened himself to God's call. On the eve of his ordination as a priest, he had put his faith in "the surprise of each day." During the darkest days of his exile in Córdoba, though feeling abandoned by God, he had still trusted. As archbishop of Buenos Aires, he had risked assassination by the drug mafia in order to protect his slum priests.

Now that he was pope, Francis still prayed daily for guidance, and he asked everyone he met, "Pray for me." More than anything, his purpose was to illustrate his faith through his actions. "Faith can only be communicated through witness, and that means love," he said to a gathering on the eve of Pentecost, 2013. "It's not so much about speaking, but rather speaking with our whole lives."

ACKNOWLEDGMENTS

I AM GRATEFUL TO ALL WHO HELPED WITH THE writing of this book. Special appreciation to my husband, Robert J. Gormley, for connecting me with David Farrell, C.S.C., missioner in Latin America, and with the Maryknoll Missioners, especially Stephen T. DeMott, M.M. (1948–2006). Robert Ellsberg, editor-in-chief and publisher of Orbis Books, pointed me toward important research sources. Alexander Kugushev, who lived in Buenos Aires for many years, contributed valuable insights and corrections to an early draft of the manuscript. And as always, thanks to the editorial staff at Aladdin, especially Karen Nagel, for their essential work.

TIME LINE

December 17, 1936: Jorge Mario Bergoglio is born in Buenos Aires, Argentina.

1945: World War II ends.

1946: Juan Perón is elected president of Argentina.

September 21, 1953: Jorge experiences a call to the priesthood.

March 1956: Jorge enters the Buenos Aires seminary to begin training for priesthood.

August 1957: Jorge nearly dies from a lung infection.

March 11, 1958: Jorge enters the Society of Jesus, and begins a two-year novitiate.

1959–60: Jorge studies the humanities in Chile.

c. 1960: Mario Bergoglio dies of a heart attack.

1961–63: Jorge studies philosophy at the Colegio Máximo.

1962: Pope John XXIII calls the Second Vatican Council.

1964–5: Jorge teaches at the Colegio de la Inmaculada Concepción in Santa Fe.

1966: Jorge teaches at the Colegio del Salvador in Buenos Aires.

1967–69: Jorge studies theology at the Colegio Máximo.

December 13, 1969: Bergoglio is ordained a priest.

1970: Bergoglio travels to Spain for his tertianship, the final leg of his Jesuit training.

TIME LINE

1971: Bergoglio is appointed Novice Master for the Jesuits of Argentina.

April 22, 1973: Bergoglio takes his final Jesuit vows.

July 31, 1973: Bergoglio becomes Provincial of the Jesuits of Argentina.

October 1973: Juan Perón is reelected president of Argentina, then dies in 1974.

1976: The military junta, led by General Jorge Videla, seizes power in Argentina.

Jesuits Orlando Yorio and Franz Jalics are kidnapped by the military.

1978: John Paul II is elected pope.

1979: Bergoglio becomes Rector of the Colegio Máximo.

1981: Regina Bergoglio dies.

1983: The military dictatorship of Argentina ends; Raúl Alfonsín is elected president.

1986: Bergoglio's term as Rector of the Colegio Máximo ends; he is sent to Germany.

Bergoglio returns to Argentina and teaches part-time.

Emilio Mignone publishes *Church and Dictatorship*, accusing the Catholic Church (including Bergoglio) of complying with Videla's dictatorship.

1987: Bergoglio is elected Procurator of Argentine Jesuits.

1989: Carlos Menem is elected president of Argentina.

1990: Bergoglio is exiled to Córdoba to serve as an ordinary priest.

TIME LINE

1992: Cardinal Quarracino appoints Bergoglio auxiliary bishop in Buenos Aires.

1997: Bergoglio is appointed Coadjutor Archbishop of Buenos Aires.

1998: Quarracino dies; Bergoglio becomes Archbishop of Buenos Aires.

February 21, 2001: Bergoglio is made a cardinal by Pope John Paul II.

Argentina suffers a massive economic crisis.

2003: Néstor Kirchner is elected president of Argentina.

2004: Kirchner repeals amnesty for crimes committed during the military dictatorship; investigations reopen.

April 2005: John Paul II dies; Bergoglio attends the conclave in Rome to elect the new pope, Benedict XVI.

November 2005: Bergoglio is elected president of the Argentine Bishops' Conference.

2007: At the Latin American bishops' conference in Aparecida, Brazil, Bergoglio writes a key document.

Néstor Kirchner dies; Cristina Kirchner becomes president of Argentina.

2010: Bergoglio testifies as a witness in the investigation of crimes committed during the Dirty War.

February 28, 2013: Pope Benedict XVI resigns.

March 13, 2013: Jorge Bergoglio is elected pope and takes the name Francis.

July 2013: Francis visits the island of Lampedusa to mourn the deaths of refugees.

Francis travels to Brazil for World Youth Day.

TIME LINE

November 2013: Francis publishes *Evangelii Gaudium*.

February 2014: Francis creates nineteen new cardinals, including many from Third World countries.

May 2014: Francis visits the Holy Land: Jordan, Palestine, Jerusalem.

June 2015: Francis publishes *Laudato si'*, an encyclical on the environment and climate change.

September 2015: Francis visits the United States.

February 2016: Francis visits Mexico and prays for immigrants at the U.S. border.

July 2016: Francis visits Poland for World Youth Day and also visits Auschwitz.

May 2017: Francis meets with the new US president, Donald Trump, and gives him a copy of *Laudato si'*.

SOURCES

BOOKS

Allen, John L. *The Francis Miracle: Inside the Transformation of the Pope and the Church*. New York: Time Books, 2015.

Bergoglio, Jorge Mario/Pope Francis. *Morning Homilies I and II*. Short daily sermons in the chapel of Santa Marta, where he lives.

_____. *Evangelii Gaudium* (*The Joy of the Gospels*). Encyclical on the Church's primary mission of evangelization in the modern world.

_____. *Laudato Si'* (*Praise Be*). Encyclical on the environment.

_____. *The Name of God Is Mercy*. New York: Random House, 2016.

Bergoglio, Jorge Mario and Abraham Skorka. *On Heaven and Earth: Pope Francis on Faith, Family, and the Church in the Twenty-First Century*. New York: Image, a Division of Penguin Random House, Inc., 2015.

Brown, Jonathan. *A Brief History of Argentina*. New York: Facts on File, 2003.

Cámara, Javier and Sebastián Pfaffen. *Understanding Pope Francis: Key Moments in the Formation of Jorge Bergoglio as a Jesuit*. CreateSpace, an amazon.com company.

Glazier, Michael and Monika K. Hellwig, eds. *The Modern Catholic Encyclopedia*. Collegeville, Minnesota: The Liturgical Press, 1994.

Hebblethwaite, Peter. *John XXIII: Pope of the Council*. Glasgow: Harper-Collins, 1994.

Ivereigh, Austen. *The Great Reformer: Francis and the Making of a Radical Pope*. New York: Henry Holt and Company, 2014.

SOURCES

Lowney, Chris. *Pope Francis: Why He Leads the Way He Leads*. Chicago: Loyola Press, 2013.

Page, Joseph A. *Perón: A Biography*. New York: Random House, 1983.

Piqué, Elisabetta. *Pope Francis: Life and Revolution*. Chicago: Loyola Press, 2014.

Tornielli, Andrea. *Francis: Pope of a New World*. San Francisco: Ignatius Press, 2013.

Vallely, Paul. *Pope Francis: Untying the Knots; The Struggle for the Soul of Catholicism*. New York: Bloomsbury, 2015.

Willey, David. *The Promise of Francis: The Man, the Pope, and the Challenge of Change*. New York: Gallery Books, 2015.

MAGAZINES AND NEWSPAPERS

Allen, John L., Jr. "Francis, Benedict More Partnership Than Rivalry." *Boston Sunday Globe*, March 20, 2016.

_____. "Pontifical Prognostication." *Boston Sunday Globe,* December 6, 2015.

_____. "Pope's Sister: Francis 'Plenty Tough Enough' to Lead." *National Catholic Reporter* (http://ncronline.org), April 3, 2013.

Berendt, Joanna. "Pope Francis, Visiting Auschwitz, Asks God for the 'Grace to Cry.'" *New York Times*, July 29, 2016.

D'Emilio, Frances. "Pope Urges Youth to Not Be Passive." *New York Times*, July 31, 2016.

Draper, Robert, and Dave Voder. "Will the Pope Change the Vatican? Or Will the Vatican Change the Pope?" *National Geographic*, August 2015.

Reel, Monte. "In Buenos Aires, 'Neighborhoods of Misery.'" *Washington Post*, April 29, 2007.

Spadaro, Antonio, SJ. "A Big Heart Open to God: The Exclusive Interview with Pope Francis." *America*, September 30, 2013.

SOURCES

Yardley, Jim, and Azam Ahmed. "Francis, at Border, Weighs In on American Debate Over Immigration." *New York Times*, February 18, 2016.

Yardley, Jim, and Laurie Goodstein. "Francis Signals a Path to Return for the Divorced." *New York Times*, April 9, 2016.

INTERNET

BBC News. "How many Roman Catholics are there in the world?" www.bbc.com/news/world-21443313, March 14, 2013.

http://news.bbc.co.uk/2/hi/americas/110016.stm. "'Dirty War' arrest." June 10, 1998.

Catholic Climate Covenant. *Care for Creation, Care for the Poor.* Highlights of *Laudato Si'*, Pope Francis's encyclical letter on ecology. www.CatholicClimateCovenant.org, June 2015.

Del Carril, Santiago. "Human rights lawyer, pope's confidant Alicia Oliveira dies." http://Buenosairesherald.com, November 6, 2014.

Glatz, Carol. "Despite close ties, pope skipped family barbecues to minister in slums." Catholic News Service. http://catholicphilly.com, March 22, 2013.

www.ignatianspirituality.com. Introduction to the main ideas of Ignatian spirituality, such as *discernment*.

https://madresdemayo.wordpress.com/las-madres/las-madres/. The Mothers of the Plaza de Mayo website.

Nicosia, Gisela. "The nephew of Pope makes the pilgrimage to the Basilica of Lujan and says he sees his uncle rejuvenated." Perfil.com, October 6, 2014.

The Pew Research Center. "Religion in Latin America: Widespread Change in a Historically Catholic Region." http://www.pewforum.org/2014/11/13/religion-in-latin-america, November 13, 2014.

Puga, Kristina. "The Bergoglios react to having a pope in the family." http://NBCLatino.com/category/people, March 14, 2013.

SOURCES

Reese, Thomas. "Does Pope Francis have a master's degree in chemistry?" National Catholic Reporter (http://ncronline.org), June 3, 2015.

http://www.usccb.org/beliefs-and-teachings/what-we-believe/index.cfm. The United States Conference of Catholic Bishops website.

www.vatican.va. The official site of the Vatican, with many speeches, letters, homilies, etc. by Pope Francis.

Vatican Insider staff. "Fr. Scannone: 'Meet my pupil, Bergoglio.'" La Stampa (www.lastampa.it/2013/04/03/vaticaninsider/eng/world-news/fr-scannone-meet-my-pupil-bergoglio-VoR9SAxaN2C5OMXVseRfzI/pagina.html), March 4, 2013.

VIDEOS

Chiamatemi Francesco (Call Me Francis). Directed by Daniele Luchetti. Italy: Taodue, Mediaset, 2015. 98 minutes. A dramatized biopic of Jorge Bergoglio.

The Francis Effect. Salt & Light Catholic Media, 2014. Documentary about the extraordinary effect of Jorge Bergoglio on the Catholic Church and beyond since his election as pope.

Secrets of the Vatican. Frontline, 2014. 85 minutes. Documentary on the clergy sexual abuse scandal and cover-up.

Mercedes Sosa: The Voice of Latin America. Argentina, 2013. 1 hour, 33 minutes. Documentary bio of hugely popular Argentine folk/protest singer.

The Mothers of Plaza de Mayo. Argentina, 1985. 64 minutes. Documentary about the group protesting the kidnapping of their children by the military dictatorship.

Our Disappeared (Nuestros Desparedicos). Argentina, 2008. 1 hour, 39 minutes. Documentary by Juan Mandelbaum, who returns to Argentina, years after fleeing the Dirty War, to interview friends and families of the "disappeared" he used to know.

SOURCES

Adolfo Perez Esquivel: Rivers of Hope. Produced by the PeaceJam Foundation, 2015. Documentary about the life of the Nobel Peace Prize Laureate Esquivel and the political turmoil in Argentina, 1931–2014.

The Dignity of the Nobodies. Directed by Fernando Solanas. Argentina, 2005. 2 hours. Documentary about the protests and riots of 2001 in Argentina in reaction to economic depression, widespread unemployment, and runaway national debt.

Spoils of War. Produced and directed by David Blaustein. Argentina, 2000. 118 minutes. Documentary about the Grandmothers of the Plaza de Mayo. Interviews with several of the grandmothers and their corresponding found grandchildren; film footage of Dirty War era.

The Mission. Directed by Roland Joffe. 1986. 2 hours, 6 minutes. Historical drama set in eighteenth-century South America. A Jesuit missionary struggles to protect his Guarani settlement from Spanish and Portuguese colonists.

INDEX

INDEX

INDEX